Contents

Cover Photo: The Umbrella, Culver City, designed by Eric Owen Moss Architects. Photo © Erhard Pfeiffer
Back Cover Illustration: Chair sketches © Frank O. Gehry

Introduction

This is the third, revised edition of a pocket directory (first published in 1994 as the *Architects Guide to Los Angeles*) that invites you to explore over 700 remarkable buildings, interiors, design resources, and arts facilities from downtown LA to the ocean, from Pasadena to Orange County, plus excursions to Santa Barbara, Palm Springs and San Diego. Each entry can be viewed from the street or visited—during regular business hours or by appointment. The intent is to provide a cross section of the best classic, contextual, and cutting-edge architecture, with a special emphasis on adventurous work of the past two decades. Well-designed hotels, restaurants, art galleries, and specialty stores of quality take their place alongside other building types.

Like any metropolis, Los Angeles is too contradictory to be comprehended at first sight. From the air or the freeway, it appears bewilderingly vast and featureless: a 450 square mile patchwork of hills, flatlands, and independent municipalities extending over five counties. Only when you begin exploring the distinctive neighborhoods do you discover its treasures and curiosities, its bizarre and felicitous juxtapositions of buildings and landscape. For the past century, it has attracted a steady stream of ambitious and talented architects, some to make an international reputation, others to languish in obscurity. LA is resilient enough to bounce back from recession, riots, and natural disasters to regain the momentum it has enjoyed before. But it has failed to make best use of its design resources; in the public and commercial realm, the city remains depressingly provincial. A secondary purpose of this guide is to draw attention to the independent artists and entrepreneurs who could change things, and to celebrate inventiveness—no matter how small the scale.

LA may disappoint its admirers (as it confounds its detractors), but it still has more to delight the persistent explorer than most American cities. Listed here are buildings of every type that respond creatively to program, site, climate, and budget. High walls and dense vegetation conceal many of the best houses, but this guide will lead you to Craftsman bungalows, post-war Case Study houses, inspired reinterpretations of the past, and experiments by several generations of modernists. Here are the must sees—from the Bradbury Building to the Getty Center, and over three decades of work by Frank Gehry— alongside follies and entertaining kitsch. Loft conversion, for cutting edge companies, has become a growth industry and is given its due. Omitted, for lack of space, are many buildings of character and value, but room has been found for places to buy outstanding books and furniture, fabrics and hardware—plus a selection of the better art, craft, and photo galleries. Another major plus in this new edition is the Art & Design Resource List, which overlaps and supplements the individual entries.

Many friends made valuable suggestions, especially to the Resource List and on outlying areas. Sincere thanks to Christine Anderson, Frances Anderton, Pamela Burton, William W. Ellinger III, Francesca Garcia Marques, Scott Johnson, Katie Klapper, Lisa Krohn, Coralie Langston-Jones, Tony Merchell, Barton & Vicki Myers, Merry Norris, Danette Riddle, Arnold Schwartzman, Tim Street Porter & Annie Kelly, Julie Taylor, Barbara Thornburg, Joni Weyl, Margery Wheaton and Bettye Young. However, the author assumes full responsibility for the selection, any errors, and all opinions expressed here.

—Michael Webb

Visiting Los Angeles

When to go It can be warm and sunny at any time of year; however, occasional rain is likely from January though March, sea mist from April through June, and hot, smoggy days in summer. Mild, dry, clear days are most common October through December.

Where to stay West Hollywood, Beverly Hills and Santa Monica offer the widest choice of accommodations, lively streets, and a little night life. Stay downtown only if you have business there and are willing to pay the price.

Getting around From Los Angeles International Airport (LAX), a taxi to downtown or the Westside is likely to cost about $25. There is frequent shuttle bus service to major hotels and outlying destinations. If your visit is limited to downtown, you can get around by Dash shuttle and taxi. The Metro Red Line links downtown to North Hollywood with many useful stops along the way, and the Blue Line light rail runs from downtown to Long Beach. However, if you plan to explore the city extensively, a car is essential; bus service is limited, and taxis are ruinously expensive over long distances—if you can find them. Reserve in advance for the best prices on a rental car. Enterprise (800 325 8007; limited hours) has some of the lowest rates; Rent-a-Wreck (800 423 2158) maintains a fleet of convertibles and vintage cars with character, though their rates have increased sharply in recent years.

Before tackling the freeways, study the map to plan your exit, and watch out for the driver working his cell phone in the fast track who abruptly cuts across four lanes to the off ramp. The average speed is about 10 mph over the limit, but don't push your luck, and never provoke another driver. Avoid the freeways at rush hours. On surface streets, you can turn right on red (except where marked). Most drivers accelerate on orange. Always stop for pedestrians—who are considered an endangered species; however, when you are walking, you should cross only at a light, marked crossing or street intersection—or you risk a fine for jaywalking.

A dependable public service in LA is the prompt delivery of parking tickets, and there are a dozen ways to err. Read all signs; many streets are reserved for residents or street cleaning at certain hours. All good restaurants offer valet parking for around $3. Many businesses and stores will validate parking on the nearest lot, and there are low evening and weekend rates even in the busiest areas.

Where to eat Listed here are restaurants at all price levels that are satisfying to the eye and the palate—call to check hours and make reservations. LA also has an extraordinary variety of plain, inexpensive storefront restaurants serving outstanding Latino, Asian, and eclectic fare. Little Tokyo, Koreatown, and other ethnic neighborhoods around downtown offer the best choice. Bohemian coffee houses provide late hours and congenial company all over the city, but especially in Midtown, West Hollywood, and Venice.

Further reading The indispensable guide is *The Architecture of Los Angeles* by David Gebhard and Robert Winter (Peregrine Smith, revised edition 1994). *The City Observed: Los Angeles* by Charles Moore, Peter Becker and Regula Campbell (Vintage Books, 1984) is full of perceptive observations. Good pictorial surveys include *Freestyle* and *The Los Angeles House*, by Tim Street Porter; Elizabeth McMillian's *Casa California*, and Adele Cygelman's *Palm Springs Modern*. For background, read the classic *Southern California: an Island on the Land* by Carey McWilliams (Peregrine Smith, 1944/1973) and Reyner Banham's *Los Angeles: the Architecture of Four Ecologies* (Penguin, 1971).

There is a wide choice of books on modern architects, beginning with Esther McCoy's *Five California Architects* and *The Second Generation*. Key monographs include *Richard Neutra and the Search for Modern Architecture* and *Irving Gill and the Architecture of Reform*, both by Thomas Hines; Judith Sheine's pocket guide *R. M. Schindler*; Alan Weintraub's *Lloyd Wright*; Frank Escher's *John Lautner, Architect*; Karen Hudson's *Paul Williams*; and the Monacelli tome, *Frank O. Gehry*. Every contemporary architect of note now has a monograph; check the list of specialized outlets.

Among periodicals, the revival of *LA Architect* as a bimonthly is encouraging news, but there is still far too little serious coverage of regional architecture and design as compared with other major cities, and LA badly needs a museum showcase/collection to match those of MoMA in New York and SFMOMA up north.

Don't leave LA without taking a whale-watching boat trip (December-March); enjoying a concert at the Hollywood Bowl (June-September); lunching in a sunny patio in mid-winter and trying not to gloat; exploring beaches, mountains, and deserts at any season; discovering that Angelenos do walk—notably on Broadway, the Venice Boardwalk and the 3rd Street Promenade—bike, and jog as well as drive.

Until 1887, when a railroad price war set off a land boom, the entire population of LA lived within walking distance of the original plaza. Now there are many commuters but few residents downtown—which is sharply divided between the towers of finance flanking the Harbor Freeway, the markets on the eastern edge, and sandwiched in between, the civic, arts, and commercial zones, plus the enclaves of Chinatown and Little Tokyo. City authorities and developers have pumped in billions of dollars to increase the relevance of downtown to the rest of LA—with little success; Ira Yellin, Tom Gilmore, and other visionaries are struggling against the odds to revitalize the city's rich historical legacy. Meanwhile, there is much to see—preferably on weekends, when most streets are traffic-free and parking becomes affordable. You can even use the DASH shuttle bus or take the Metro.

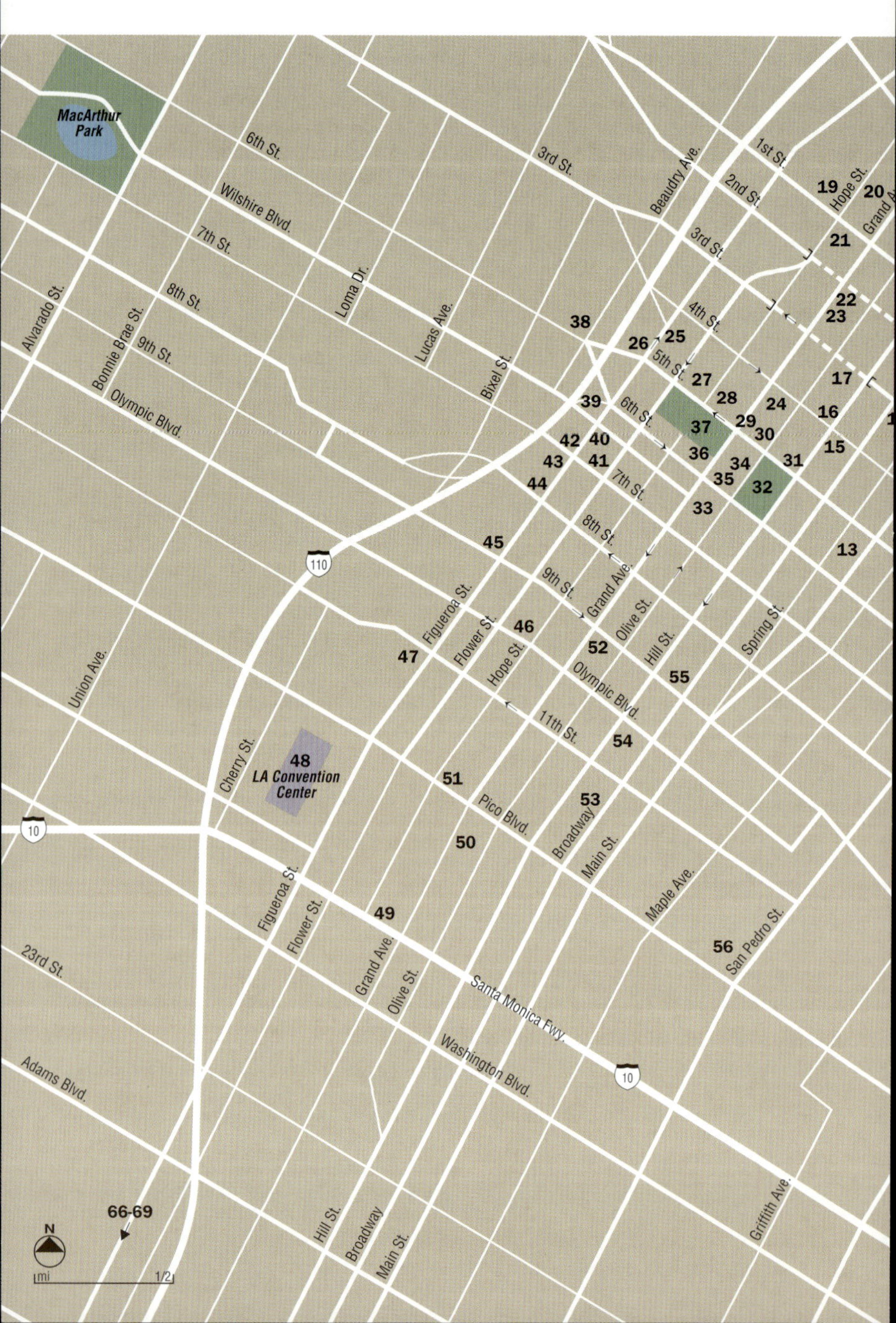

1 **Union Station** (1939, John & Donald Parkinson) Glorious moderne version of a Spanish Mission, last built of the great American railroad terminals, which has been restored and redeveloped by Catellus Development to serve as the hub of an integrated public transit system. Spilling out into the arched concourse is **Traxx** (1997, Rogerio Carvalhiero), a sleek new restaurant acclaimed for Tara Thomas's gutsy American food. At night or for lunch in the jacaranda shaded patio, it is the most romantic place in LA. Free valet parking. 800 N. Alameda St. 213 625 1999

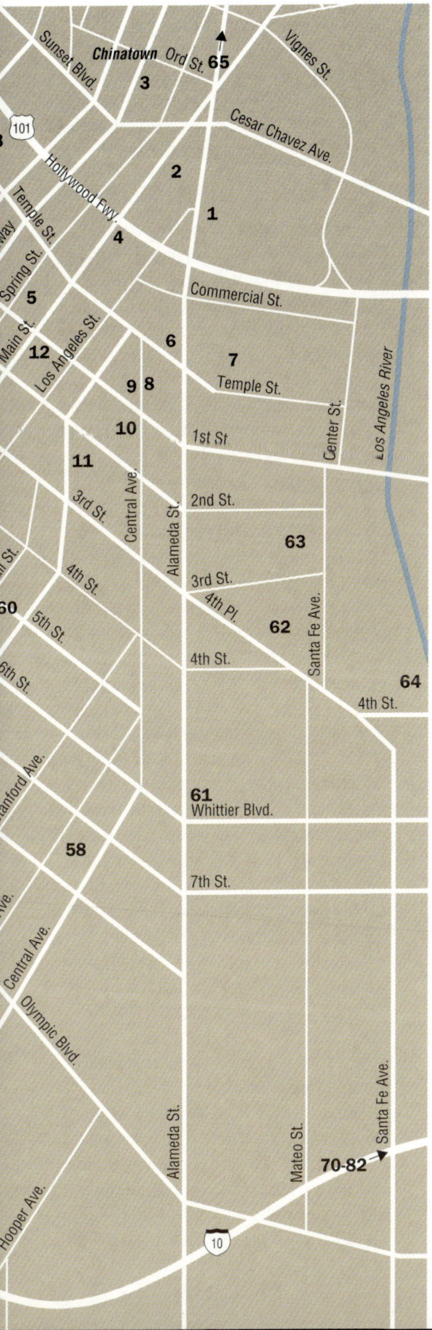

1 **MetroRail Red Line** 17 costly miles of underground track link Union Station to the Civic Center (1st & Hill), Pershing Square (5th & Hill), Metro Center (7th & Flower; terminus of the Blue Line light rail), Westlake-McArthur Park, and Wilshire-Vermont. From here, one branch extends to Wilshire & Western, another runs north on Vermont, west on Hollywood to Highland, and on to Universal City and North Hollywood. Sadly, few of the 12 stations are notable for their architecture or art. Information: 800 266 6883

2 **El Pueblo de Los Angeles** Across the street from Union Station are the over-restored 19th century relics of the original settlement, plaza, and touristy Olvera Street with its Mexican craft and food stands. For a fast bite, try the funky **Philippe The Original** at 1001 N. Alameda St. 213 628 3781

3 **Chinatown** The original Chinese settlement was relocated in the late '30s from the site of Union Station to this *Chu Chin Chow* stage set with its neon-outlined pagoda and exaggerated ornament. Centered on North Broadway at Ord St. Recommended restaurants include **Mon Kee** (679 N. Spring St, 213 628 6717) and **Ocean Seafood** (750 N. Hill St, 213 687 3088). Better ones, including **Ocean Star** (145 N. Atlantic Ave, 626 308 2128) and **Lake Spring** (219 E. Garvey Ave, 626 280 3571) are in Monterey Park, the new center of Chinese immigration, 10 miles E. of downtown.

3 **China Art Objects** (1999, Pae) Giovanni Intra shows work by young and established LA artists such as Jorge Pardo and Rudy Bust in a gallery that joins other pioneers (including the **Black Dragon Society** and **Goldman Trevis**) on this new frontier for art. W-Sa, noon-6pm. 933 Chung King Rd, off N. Hill St. 213 613 0384

4 **Pedestrian Bridge Project** (1999, Morphosis) Architecture as art: a bold proposal, as yet unfunded, for a walkway over the Hollywood Fwy. at Main St, linking the Pueblo to the Civic Center. The steel frame would support electronic billboards and a restaurant above a bougainvillea shaded deck.

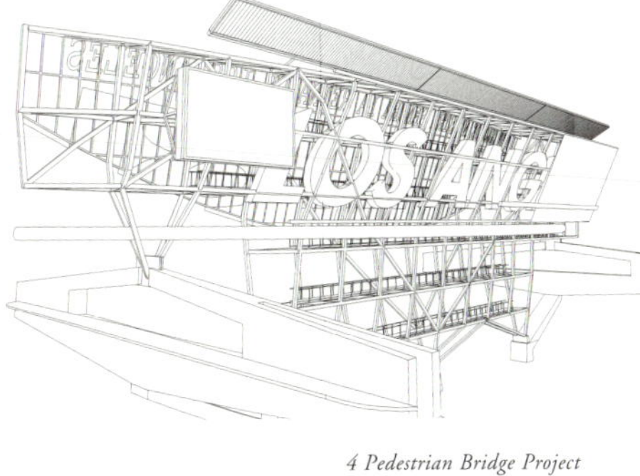

4 Pedestrian Bridge Project

5 City Hall (1928, Austin, Parkinson, Martin, Whittlesey) Monumental, pyramid-capped tower; until 1957, it was the only exception to the city's 13 story height limit. The 27th floor observation deck is currently closed for seismic upgrading, but the marble rotunda and halls, restored by Hardy Holzman Pfeiffer, can still be seen. 200 N. Spring St.

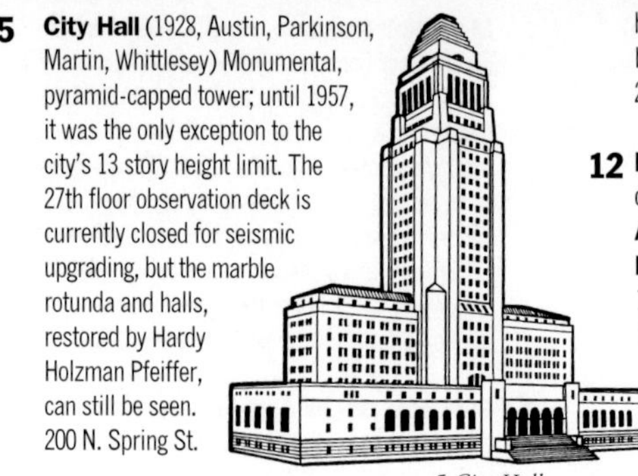

5 City Hall

6 LA Metropolitan Detention Center (1988, Ellerbe Becket/Louis Naidorf) Cool white 13 story tower with slit windows and outdoor recreation decks that mute the impact of this 588 bed, maximum security facility. 635 N. Alameda St. The Jonathan Borofsky sculpture of four men perforated with bullet holes (on the plaza of the Federal Courts Building) offers an ironic commentary. 255 E. Temple St.

6 Veterans Administration Outpatient Clinic (1992, BTA) Sleek exterior clad in granite and aluminum, tailored to the sharply angled site; flexible, user-friendly interiors. A model of how to make a huge, complex facility responsive to its users and the street. E. Temple & N. Alameda Sts.

7 DWP Central District HQ, Phase II (1992, Barton Phelps & Associates with Clements & Clements) Boldly modeled forms in enameled steel and grooved concrete give this functional facility an urban presence. 433 E. Temple St.

8 The Geffen Contemporary at MOCA (1983, Frank O. Gehry & Associates) A tough, raw-edged masterpiece, recycled from a police garage, showcases changing exhibitions of adventurous art and architecture. Tu-Su, 11am-5pm; Th til 8pm. 152 N. Central Ave. 213 626 6222

9 Japanese American National Museum (1925, Edgar Cline; remodeled 1992, KNSU Joint Venture Architects) Imaginative conversion of a reinforced concrete Buddhist temple. 119 N. Central Ave. 213 625 0414. Across the street is a new pavilion (1996, Gyo Obata/HOK) housing the resource center, permanent collection, and exhibition galleries. The glass rotunda and external cladding of red sandstone are too slick.

10 Japanese Village Plaza Mall (1979) Commercial hub of Little Tokyo. A firemen's lookout tower, blue tile roofs, white stucco walls, and decorative landscaping make this an agreeable place to shop, eat, or stroll. 1st St. at Central Ave.

11 Japanese American Cultural and Community Center (1983, Kajima Associates with George Shinno) Library, bookstore, chamber theater hosting a lively arts program, and plaza with an Isamu Noguchi rock sculpture. 244 S. San Pedro St. 213 628 2725

12 New Otani Hotel East meets West in this Japanese-owned hotel, much patronized by business travelers. **A Thousand Cranes** restaurant and the **Genji Bar** on the 4th floor overlook a delightful roof garden. 1st at S. Los Angeles Sts. 213 253 9255. In the ground floor shopping arcade is **Kinokuniya** (213 687 4480), a useful source for English language books on Japan.

South Spring Street, once known as the Wall Street of the West, is full of early 20th century gems awaiting a new role. Developer Tom Gilmore has launched the **Old Bank District**, converting the buildings on the south side of 4th St. between Spring and Main Sts. into loft apartments, with neighborhood shops at street level.

13 LA Theatre Center (1916, John Parkinson; remodeled 1985, John Sergio Fisher & Associates) Four small, steeply raked auditoria lead out of what was originally a banking hall; modern and classical details, intimate and grand spaces are deftly interwoven. 514 S. Spring St. 213 627 6500

South Broadway, 3rd St. to Olympic Blvd. Before 1950, this was LA's commercial and entertainment hub; today, it's the Latino Main Street, unkempt, but pulsing with the street life missing from the rest of downtown. This is the first and largest **Historic Theater District** in the US; one of the LA Conservancy's 12 Saturday morning walking tours will get you into the major movie palaces, and there's a summer series of special events. The LAC has an ambitious plan to leverage public and private investment in order to revitalize the district as a residential and entertainment zone. Information: 213 623 2489

Highlights include the **Million Dollar** (1918, Albert C. Martin & William Woollett; restored 1994, Levin & Associates/Denny Lord for developer Ira Yellin) with its exuberant facade, baroque auditorium—now used as a church, and residential floors above (#307); **Los Angeles** (1931, S. Charles Lee), a masterly exercise in French baroque, inspired by Versailles, that brilliantly exploits its narrow site (# 615); **Orpheum** (1926, G. Albert Landsburg), an opulent marble lobby and French baroque auditorium (#842); **United Artists** (1926, Walker & Eisen), a Spanish Gothic cathedral, aptly reused as a church (#929).

Other attractions include the ebullient **Grand Central Public Market** (#317, 213 624 2378), also restored by Levin & Associates for Ira Yellin, selling food of every kind, and a handsome new parking garage in back; the 3-story **Broadway Spring Arcade** (#542); and **Clifton's Brookdale Cafeteria**, with its sidewalk terrazzo medallions and atmospheric interior with stuffed moose (#648).

Black: exterior only, or open to public **Blue:** interior; by appt. only **Red:** private residence, do not disturb **Green:** park, or public open space

14 Bradbury Building (1893, George Wyman; restored 1991, Levin & Associates) Behind a plain brick facade is LA's greatest interior. Offices are ranged around a skylit atrium with dark ironwork, tiled stairs, polished wood, and open-cage elevators. Lobby open to public during business hours. 304 S. Broadway. 213 626 1893 In back is **Biddy Mason Park,** with a memorial wall by Sheila de Bretteville & Dolores Hayden, and landscaping by Burton & Spitz.

15 Junipero Serra State Office Building (1914; remodeled 2000, Johnson Fain Partners) The handsome facade of the former Broadway department store has been restored; the interior converted to use by state employees. 320 W. 4th St.

16 Angel's Flight (1901; restored 1996, Tetra Design) Short funicular railway that originally carried residents of Bunker Hill to their offices down-town, reconstructed as a picturesque joy ride after 27 years in storage. Landscaped plaza by Public Works. 351 S. Hill St.

17 Angelus Plaza (1981, Dworsky Associates) Humane housing for seniors. The poured concrete apartments step up Bunker Hill, giving each a terrace and a view of greenery. S. Hill St, between 2nd and 4th Sts.

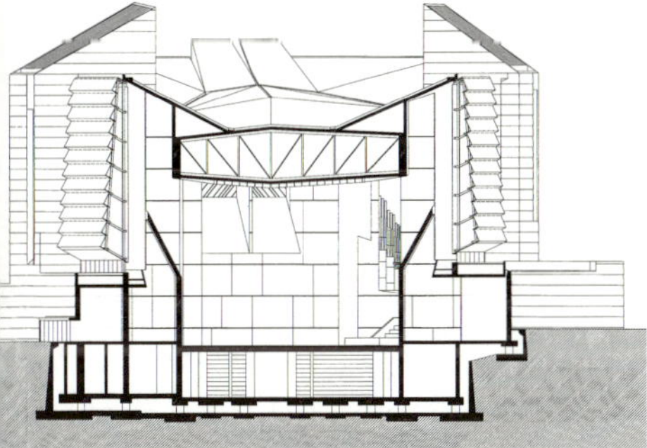

18 Cathedral of Our Lady of the Angels

18 Cathedral of Our Lady of the Angels (1996-2002, Jose Rafael Moneo with Leo A. Daly) In his West Coast debut, Moneo has created one of the great modern worship spaces, infusing a dynamic exposed concrete structure with light and spirituality. The interior will seat 3000; another 6000 will be able to gather on the plaza with its fountain by Lita Albuquerque. N. Grand Ave. between Grand Ave. and Hill St, Temple St. and Fwy 101. Tom Gilmore has bought **St. Vibiana's**, the old cathedral at 2nd & S. Main Sts, and hopes to turn it into a performing arts facility with a new library in back.

19 Department of Water & Power HQ (1965, Albert C. Martin & Associates) Elegantly stacked floor planes, best seen when lit up at night. 111 N. Hope St.

20 Performing Arts Center of Los Angeles County (1969, Welton Becket & Associates) Formerly known as the Music Center. The cavernous **Dorothy Chandler Pavilion** presents classical music and opera; road shows are staged in the remodeled **Ahmanson Theatre**; adventurous repertory in the **Mark Taper Forum**. All are perched atop a podium with parking below. The bleak plaza with its fountains by WET and its Lipschitz bronze is to be improved. Grand Ave, between W. Temple and 1st St. 213 972 7211

21 Walt Disney Concert Hall

21 Walt Disney Concert Hall (1988-2002, Frank O. Gehry & Associates) Construction is finally under way on this inspiring civic symbol, which will enhance the playing and the experience of hearing the LA Philharmonic. Billowing sails of stainless steel will wrap the 2390 seat auditorium, foyer, reception, and rehearsal spaces. Below is a separate theater for CalArts. Gardens and outdoor amphitheaters will help integrate the hall with the life of the city. S. Grand Ave, between 1st & 2nd Sts.

California Plaza Sterile memorial to "urban renewal." In the late '50s, the Community Redevelopment Agency (CRA) flattened Bunker Hill and bulldozed its Victorian mansions and decrepit rooming houses. In 1980, CRA compounded its error by selecting the bland Cadillac Fairview/Arthur Erickson proposal for the last undeveloped parcel, in preference to Maguire Thomas Partners' scheme for a lively urban mix that would have animated the now deserted streets. Bounded by 2nd & 4th, S. Grand & Hill Sts.

22 The Colburn School of Performing Arts (1998, Hardy Holzman Pfeiffer Associates) A three level complex of music and dance studios, broad concourses, and the 420 seat **Zipper Concert Hall** are linked by a skylit staircase. Reticent facade of Roman brick and zinc scales, elegantly curved wood and plexi screens within, and—a remarkable treasure—the reconstructed **Jascha Heifetz Studio** (1946, Lloyd Wright) which adjoined the celebrated violist's house in West LA. 200 S. Grand Ave. 213 621 2200

23 Museum of Contemporary Art/MOCA (1986-1997, Arata Isozaki with Gruen Associates) A cluster of Platonic solids, clad in rough textured, red sandstone, hunkered down amid the office towers. Major art and architecture exhibitions are presented in skylit galleries leading off the sunken court, to which Isozaki recently added an airy canopy to shade the **Patinette** cafe. Excellent book & gift store. Tu-Su, 11am-5pm; Th till 8pm. 250 S. Grand Ave. 213 621 2766

24 Wells Fargo Center (1982-84, Marc Goldstein/ Skidmore, Owings & Merrill) Twin trapezoidal granite-clad towers flank an art and restaurant filled garden court by Lawrence Halprin & Allen Fong. 350 S. Hope St. Opening off the elevated plaza is:

24 Nick + Stef's (1999, Belzberg Architects) Folded maple soffits, angled room dividers, and elegant leather booths and armchairs warm a cavernous space and give a fresh spin to the traditional steak house. The well-aged meat is superbly prepared. 330 S. Hope St. 213 680 0330

25 Westin Bonaventure Hotel (1976, John Portman) Five mirror-glass silos that appear as a flashy bauble from the freeway; however, the concrete base shuns the street. A maze of restaurants, public and guest rooms lead out of the predictable atrium. 404 S. Figueroa St. 213 624 1000

26 Ciudad (1998, Schweitzer BIM) Inventive Latin food in a cubist extravaganza with Miro-inspired murals and sunny colors to compensate for the absence of natural light. 445 S. Figueroa St. 213 486 5171

27 444 S. Flower Building The palm shaded forecourt on Flower St. is linked by steps and escalators to Bunker Hill Steps. Along the way are art works by Mark DiSuvero, Michael Heizer, Frank Stella, Bruce Nauman and Robert Rauschenberg.

28 First Interstate World Center (1989, Pei, Cobb, Freed & Partners/Harold Fredenburg) Orthogonal and circular geometries are interwoven in this 1017 ft. tower, the tallest building on the West Coast. It successfully crowns the downtown skyline, but becomes less impressive the closer you get. Lobby relief by Vitaly Komar and Alexander Melamid. Wrapped around the west side of the tower are the **Bunker Hill Steps** (1990, Lawrence Halprin), a pedestrian link—distantly inspired by the Spanish Steps in Rome—with escalators, greenery, a cascade, and cafes. Opening off the first-level terrace is the **Herman Miller** contract furnishings showroom. 633 W. 5th St. 213 627 5900

29 One Bunker Hill (1931, Allison & Allison) Well-restored zig zag moderne office tower, dwarfed by its neighbors, with lobby mural by Hugo Ballin. S. Grand Ave at W. 5th St.

30 The Gas Company (1991, Richard Keating/ Skidmore, Owings & Merrill) Sleek 52 story tower has a distinctive blue glass crown that symbolizes a gas flame, and a handsome raised lobby that leads to a fountain court and a disappointing Richard Stella mural at the rear of the building. 555 W. 5th St.

31 Title Guarantee Building (1931, John & Donald Parkinson) Zig zag tower, with a Gothic crown, a Ballin mural in the lobby, and a Metro entrance below. W. 5th at Hill St.

32 Pershing Square (1992-94, Ricardo Legorreta & Hanna/Olin) An impressive, though underutilized public space: this neglected park was transformed into an urban plaza through a CRA/corporate partnership, with Maguire Thomas Partners as catalysts. Sidewalks bridge parking ramps to improve access; spaces and shifts of level are subtly choreographed to lead you in and create a sense of place. Underground garage and terrace cafe. Barbara McCarren did the earthquake fissure and other art works. Varied plantings are maturing to shade and layer the square. Olive & 5th, Hill & 6th Sts.

33 Oviatt Building (1928, Walker & Eisen; restored 1980, Levin & Associates) Built as an exclusive men's store and offices. The former retail space is now **Cicada** (213 488 9488), an excellent Italian restaurant that has, regretably, tarted up the gorgeous Art Deco interior. However, the penthouse is still pure Paris 1925, and can be rented for parties. 617 S. Olive St. 213 622 6096

34 Regal Biltmore Hotel (1923, Schultze & Weaver) The high point of the grand, richly ornamented interiors is the Spanish Renaissance style **Rendezvous Court** (for breakfast, tea & cocktails). Sumptuously tiled Roman bath downstairs. Sensual Art Deco murals in the **Cognac Room**, which is open till late. 506 S. Grand Ave. 213 624 1011

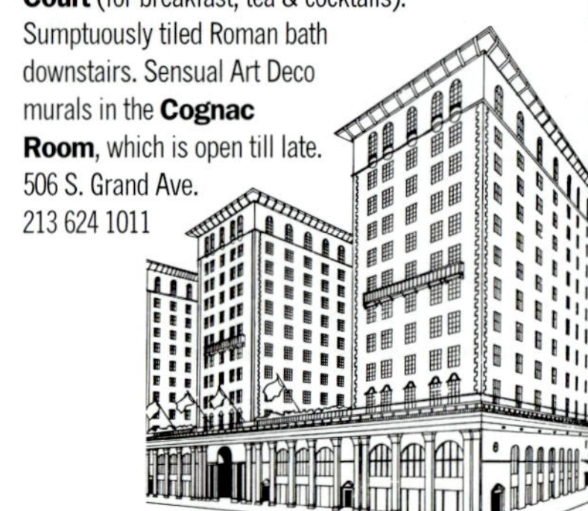

34 Regal Biltmore Hotel

35 Water Grill Great seafood in a stylish setting. 544 S. Grand Ave. 213 891 0900

36 Wyndham-Checkers (1927, Charles F. Whittlesey; remodeled 1990, Eric B. Holtsmark, Kaplan/ McLaughlin/Diaz; interiors by James Northcutt & Associates) Luxurious small hotel, with elegant, antique filled interiors, and a highly acclaimed restaurant. 535 S. Grand Ave. 213 624 0000

Black: exterior only, or open to public **Blue:** interior; by appt. only **Red:** private residence, do not disturb **Green:** park, or public open space

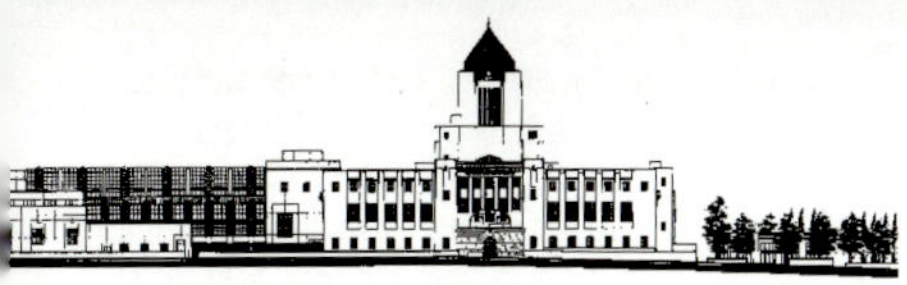

37 Central Library

37 Central Library (1922-26, Bertram Goodhue; restored and extended 1987-93, Hardy Holzman Pfeiffer Associates) Reinforced concrete landmark that combines Beaux Arts planning and exotic ornament in an inspired whole. Steps lead up from the low ceilinged entrance lobby to a soaring, muraled rotunda beneath the pyramid-capped tower. Gutted by arson in 1987, it has been brilliantly restored and more than doubled in size. New reading rooms, book stacks, and offices open off a lofty glass roofed atrium that brings natural light to the four subterranean stories. Other additions include the **Mark Taper Theater**, and atop the parking garage on the west side, the **Maguire Gardens** (1993, Lawrence Halprin), a generously landscaped pocket park that celebrates the initiative of Robert F. Maguire III in helping save the library from destruction. W. 5th St. between Flower St. & Grand Ave. Within the garden is:

37 Café Pinot (1995, interiors by Alcasar Terrell) Understated interior with mural by Hollis Rhodes, bar and leafy patio; uneven bistro fare. 700 W. 5th St. 213 239 6500

38 Los Angeles Center Studios Bay Area artist Mark Stock has revived LA's dormant tradition of quality murals with his dramatic enhancement of two new sound stages. A three part narrative will evolve over time; call for permission to walk through the gate and see the work close up. Corner of 4th & Boylston Sts. 213 891 1234

39 Sanwa Bank Plaza (1991, Albert C. Martin & Associates) 52 story office tower, set at an angle to the street corner and a triangular plaza. Illuminated green glass crown and 72 foot skylit atrium. 601 S. Figueroa St. at Wilshire Blvd. Leading out of the lobby is:

39 Pacific Grill (1993, RoTo Architects) A sharp edged interior originally commissioned by Larry Nicola. Blond wood ribs arch over the diners, Lisa Krohn's lights swoop down like exotic flowers, and there's a steel ribbed lobby terrace. 213 485 0927

40 Engine Company No 28 Recycled 1912 firehouse serving hearty food to an enthusiastic crowd. 644 S. Figueroa St. 213 624 6996

41 Fine Arts Building (1925, Walker & Eisen; restored 1986, Levin & Associates) Romanesque facade and lofty tiled lobby: another inspired rejuvenation by developer Wayne Ratkovich (Oviatt, Wiltern Center, Chapman Market, Alex Theatre). 811 W. 7th St.

42 LA Visitors Bureau M-F, 8am-5pm; Sa, 8:30am-5pm. 685 S. Figueroa St. (Hilton Hotel). 213 689 8822

43 Seventh Market Place (1985, Jerde Partnership) Stores are ranged around a sunken circular food court dressed in period decor. 735 S. Figueroa St. 213 955 7150

44 777 Tower (1991, Cesar Pelli & Associates) Sharp edged but sensuous, clad in white enameled metal, bowed out at front and back, with a soaring lobby recessed behind a portico that anchors the corner at street level. 777 S. Figueroa St.

45 Zita Trattoria & Bar (2000, CSC Architecture) Traditional Italian cuisine in a granite-clad pavilion with five pyramidal skylights. 825 W. 9th St.

46 The Oh Company (2000, BAM) Cinderblock desks and Cappellini seating set the tone of understated, monochomatic elegance with an edge. 605 W. Olympic Blvd, Suite 800. 213 622 2059

47 Staples Arena (1999, NBBJ) A huge new sports/entertainment arena, humanized by the architects' decision to wrap transparent lobbies around the seating bowl, reducing its bulk and allowing views in and out. Jennifer Steinkamp's video projection on the prow of the building adds another dimension, but the project is fatally compromised by the sponsors' crass self-promotion, using signs that belong on a strip. Figueroa at 11th St. 213 742 7100

48 LA Convention Center (1993, Pei, Cobb, Freed & Partners with Gruen Associates) On the freeway side, trucks load through a curved and canopied green glass wall; along Figueroa, two soaring steel-framed glass lobbies provide a signature for the recent addition, which conceals the original drab box. The huge interiors have an easy flow and readable signage. Alexis Smith created the terrazzo maps in the lobby floors. S. Figueroa St. between 11th St. & Venice Blvd. 213 741 1151

49 Young Apartments (1911; 1996, remodeled by Cavaedium) Exemplary renovation of a landmark apartment block to house low income tenants. Juicy classical facades, with terracotta ornament and jutting cornice, well-proportioned rooms and garden court. 1621 S. Grand Ave.

50 CIGNA Healthplan (1991, David Lawrence Gray) Sleek, steel-framed curtain-wall building, with ground floor retail/medical, four levels of parking and three of doctors' suites. 1400 S. Grand Ave.

51 Museum of Neon Art (1996, Cavaedium) Functional, low budget build-out of the ground floor of a high-rise in S. Hope Park provides spacious galleries for exhibitions, classes and archives. MONA advances the art and preserves the heritage of neon. 501 W. Olympic Blvd. 213 489 9918

52 Federal Reserve Bank of San Francisco (1988, Dworsky Associates) A sleek, granite-clad block with a bowed entrance leading to a skylit atrium. 950 S. Grand Ave.

53 Herald Examiner Building (1912, Julia Morgan) A former newspaper office in search of a new headline. There's a hint of San Simeon in this bold adaptation of Spanish tradition to contemporary uses. 1111 S. Broadway.

54 Mayan (1927, Morgan, Walls & Clements) Gaudily painted warrior priests glare down from the facade; giant figures loom through the gloom within. This former musical theater is now a night club. 1038 S. Hill St. 213 746 4287. Across the street is Kent Twitchell's multi-story mural of Ed Ruscha.

55 849 Building (1929, Claude Beelman). Gold-accented turquoise terracotta clads this landmark zig zag moderne tower. 849 S. Broadway.

56 DWP Central District HQ & Warehouse (1992, Mehrdad Yazdani/Ellerbe Becket) The spirit of the '30s Public Works Administration revived in a tough complex of color banded concrete block and glass brick. 1370 S. Wall St.

57 Coca Cola Building (1937, Robert Derrah) Streamline ocean liner wrapped around five industrial sheds. 1334 S. Central Ave.

59 Drop-in Center (1999, Lehrer Architects) City sponsored health and counseling facility with crisp white buildings ranged around three sides of a landscaped courtyard to welcome the homeless off the streets. 628 San Julian St.

60 Simone Hotel (1992, Koning Eizenberg) LA's first new SRO in 40 years stretches a tight budget to create a street-smart building that's efficient and humane. 520 San Julian St.

61 DWP Construction HQ (1992, Neil Stanton Palmer) Steel and concrete block used with power and assurance. 1212 Palmetto off Alameda St.

62 ReForm (1996, Lorcan O'Herlihy) Lively dialogue between classical moldings (left over from a 1925 bank) and minimalist screens in this showroom/ workshop for sleek, exotic furniture designed by Nancy Montgomery. 800 Traction Ave, #20. 213 680 3010

63 Southern View (1909, John Parkinson; remodeled 1988, Appleton, Melchur & Associates) Handsome brick warehouse turned mixed-use complex, with 21 artists' studio/residences. 923 E. 3rd St. Within the building on Vignes St, between 2nd & 3rd Sts. is:

63 R-23 Superb sushi and more from veterans of Katsu, served in a minimalist space with cardboard chairs and Mineo Mizuno ceramics. 213 687 7178

64 LA River The volunteer Friends of the LA River are energetically lobbying to return part of this 52 mile concrete lined watercourse to its natural state—for flood control and public recreation—and they organize tours of its historic bridges, like the handsome 4th St. span. Information: 323 223 0585

65 The Brewery An industrial complex transformed into a vibrant community of artists' studios, with a cafe and an art gallery. 642 Moulton Ave. 323 222 3001

65 Carlson-Reges House (1996, RoTo Architects) Welded steel loft jutting up from an anonymous building, sandwiched between a railroad line and The Brewery. Steel baffles reduce the roar of passing trains; a cylinder runs up through the building, enclosing a bathroom and ending in a belvedere. 698 Moulton Ave.

66 University of Southern California Includes a major architecture school, but the campus lacks noteworthy buildings. Interesting exhibitions at the **Fisher Gallery** (213 740 4561); good film programs at the luxurious **Norris Theatre** (213 740 1946). Jefferson & Exposition Blvds, Figueroa & Vermont Sts. 213 743 2311

67 Shrine Civic Auditorium (1926, John Austin, A. M. Edelman, G. Albert Landsburg) Movie set mosque, built for the Shriners, now used for occasional spectacles. 665 W. Jefferson Blvd. 213 749 5123

68 California Science Center (1998, Zimmer Gunsul Frasca Partnership) A cylindrical glass rotunda and the patterned tile facade of an Imax theater complement a wing of the old Museum of Science & Industry that survived the '94 earthquake. Figueroa at 39th Sts. 213 744 7400

69 California Aerospace Museum (1984, Frank O. Gehry & Associates) An F-104 is pinned like a butterfly above the entrance to this blank walled hangar; the interior is closed for remodeling through 2002. Exposition Blvd. at Figueroa St.

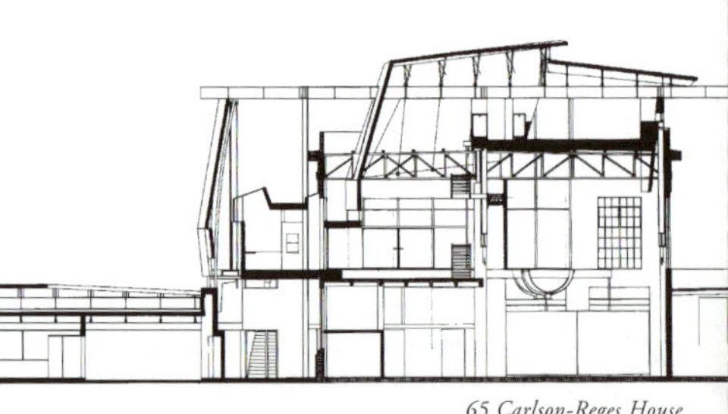

65 Carlson-Reges House

Black: exterior only, or open to public **Blue:** interior; by appt. only **Red:** private residence, do not disturb **Green:** park, or public open space

South & East of Downtown

70 Farmer John's Murals (1953, Leslie Grimes)
Pigs cavort on the walls of this meatpacking plant
thanks to a talented scene painter, and the tradition
was continued after he fell to his death. One of LA's
special places. 3049 E. Vernon Ave, east of Soto St.

71 Winnie & Sutch Co. (1939, William Myer)
Streamline concrete pylons distinguish this handsome
moderne factory. 5610 S. Soto St.

72 Thomas Jefferson High School (1937, Stiles
Clements) Epitome of streamline moderne, with a
facade that is bowed, faced, finned, and set off by
relief lettering. 1319 E. 41st St.

73 Bethlehem Baptist Church (1944, R. M.
Schindler) The architect's only religious structure is a
cutaway L plan box, De Stijl in its asymetry, with over-
lapping stucco bands outside and in, and a skylight in
the form of a cross. A tiny gem. 4900 S. Compton Ave.

77 Cerritos Center for the Performing Arts
(1993, Barton Myers Associates) Multipurpose
auditorium that can be rapidly reconfigured (by use
of hydraulic lifts and air casters) to become a 1950
seat shoebox concert hall, arena, opera house with fly
tower, intimate 950 seat theater, and level banquet/
exhibition space. Auditorium and meeting rooms are
flanked by lobbies, courtyards, and gardens to extend
spaces outdoors. April Greiman designed the brightly
colored ceramic tile patterns on the exteriors. S. on
Santa Ana Fwy, W. on Rte. 91, Shoemaker Ave. exit to
12700 Center Court Dr, Cerritos. 310 916 8510

78 SkyRose Chapel (1997, Fay Jones & Maurice
Jennings) Gothic is reborn in the traceried wooden
vault of this spacious hilltop chapel, which celebrates
life as much as it memorializes death. It is the
largest of six chapels by the acclaimed designers of
Thorncrown in rural Arkansas. Rose Hills Memorial
Park, 3888 S. Workman Mill Rd, off the 605 Fwy,
Whittier. 310 699 0921

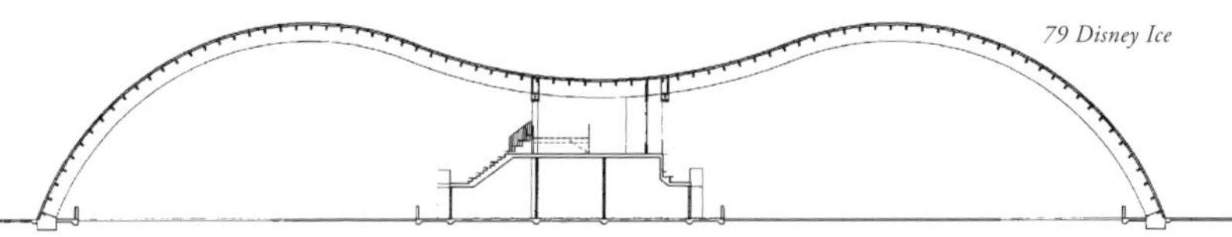

79 Disney Ice

74 Watts Towers (1921-54, Sam Rodia) A must
see: the life-work of an Italian plasterer who single-
handedly erected plaster-clad iron tracery to a height
of 100 feet, and encrusted it with shells and fragments
of china and glass. Under restoration for 20 years,
the interior may reopen for weekend visits in May
2001.The Blue Line light rail stops at 103rd St; walk
south on Graham Ave. By car, drive about six miles
south on the Harbor Fwy, E. on Century Blvd, S. on
Broadway, E. on 108th St, N. on Graham. Be aware
of the high crime rate in the area. 1765 E. 107th St.
213 485 2433

75 The Citadel (1929, Morgan, Walls & Clements;
remodeled 1990, Sussman-Prejza/Fernando Vazquez
& Scott Cuyler; office park by the Nadel Partnership;
landscaping by Martha Schwartz, Ken Smith, David
Meyer) Assyrian fortress, built as a factory for Samson
Tire. Behind the refurbished walls is a dynamic
clothing factory outlet center that juxtaposes brightly
colored frames and wall planes in forced perspective
with fragments of the original industrial sheds. 5675
Telegraph Rd, off Santa Ana Fwy, City of Commerce.

76 Oldest Surviving McDonald's (1953, Stanley C.
Meston) The LA Conservancy saved this memento
from the era when a mere 500 million hamburgers had
been sold. The parabolic curves, crisply functional
counter/kitchen, and flying wedge roof are pure '50s;
no fake mansards on this baby. The sign alone is worth
the drive and you can get an original formula milk-
shake. According to Alan Hess in *Googie*, this was the
second franchise to be built with the arches, following
a now razed example in Phoenix. S. on Santa Ana Fwy,
S. on Lakewood Blvd. to Florence Ave, Downey.

79 Disney Ice (1995, Frank O. Gehry & Associates)
Low budget functionalism. Standing seam aluminum
panels are wrapped tightly over the arched glulam
vaults of two rinks, which are separated by a concrete
core of changing rooms, bleachers, and glass walled
cafe. 300 W. Lincoln Ave, Anaheim. 714 535 7465

80 Team Disney (1995, Frank O. Gehry & Associates)
Staff offices for park employees. From the freeway,
you glimpse a corrugated berm protecting a long
four story building, clad in quilted steel shingles that
refract the light and change color as you drive by. The
private facade is clad in bright yellow stucco, broken
up by exuberant staircases and metal canopies.
800 W. Ball Rd, Anaheim.

81 Disneyland "This incredibly energetic collection
of environmental experiences offers enough lessons
for a whole architectural education in all the things
that matter," wrote Charles Moore, and if the cloying
sweetness and relentless manipulation don't choke
you, you may concede his point. S. on Santa Ana Fwy,
exit Harbor Blvd, Anaheim. 714 781 4565

82 Crystal Cathedral (1980-1990, Johnson & Burgee)
Shimmering crystalline worship space and glass tower
for an evangelist who pioneered the drive-in service.
His first modest church (1961, Richard Neutra) with
its luminous glass-walled chapel can also be seen.
To come is an aluminum-clad visitor center (2002,
Richard Meier & Partners) that will complement the
existing buildings. 12141 Lewis St, a mile south of
Disneyland, Garden Grove. 714 971 4000

The stages of LA's growth to the west are almost as clear as the rings on a tree, progressing from Queen Anne at the edge of downtown to the moderne (now giving way to modern) of Miracle Mile. Wilshire Blvd is the spine that links the economically diverse communities of midtown, from the tenements of new immigrants to the mansions of Hancock Park and the chic showrooms that border Beverly Hills and West Hollywood.

1 **Angelino Heights** LA's first commuter suburb, begun in the 1887 land boom; a streetcar once carried commuters from the base of the hill to their offices on Spring St. The 1300 block of Carroll Ave, with its Queen Anne and Eastlake houses, has been lovingly restored.

2 **Loyola Law School** (1981-87, Frank O. Gehry & Associates) Inspired by Jefferson's "Academical Village" and designed to promote social intercourse, this urban campus employs classical references and forced perspective to animate a confined site. A copper-clad chapel faces moot hall across the courtyard, which includes Claes Oldenburg's *Toppling*

Ladder. Classrooms are stacked in a long stucco block with an exterior stair, enclosing the campus to the west. Recent additions include a parking structure, and to come, a mock court with a silvery arched roof. 1441 W. Olympic Blvd. 323 736 1000

3 **Camino Nuevo Charter Academy** (2000, Daly Genik) Brilliant recycling of a typically ugly mini mall into a progressive K-5 school. The architects stripped the facade, added a steel frame, and wrapped it to create pockets of indoor and outdoor teaching space. The parking lot becomes a playground, separated from the street by a serrated row of restrooms. 697 S. Burlington Ave.

4 **Bonnie Brae Victorians** A slightly grander version of Angelino Heights—though with more gaps —includes a couple of Newsom's splendidly confident Queen Anne mansions. 800 and 1000 blocks of S. Bonnie Brae St.

5 **St. Vincent de Paul** (1925, Albert C. Martin) Churrigueresque church with tiled dome, built when this was a fashionable residential neighborhood. To the south is the **Automobile Club of Southern**

California (1923, Hunt & Burns/Roland E. Coate), an exuberant Spanish Colonial pile with an impressive courtyard. S. Figueroa at W. Adams Blvd.

6 Park Plaza Hotel (1924, Curlett & Beelman) Former Elks Lodge, notable for its massing and large sculptured figures (recalling Goodhue's Central Library) and for Anthony B. Heinsbergen's interiors. 607 S. Park View St. 213 384 5281

7 Mid-Wilshire Neon Thanks to Adolfo Nodal, general manager of the LA Cultural Affairs Dept, owners of vintage apartment towers have been persuaded to relight their rooftop neon signs, adding color and life to this depressed neighborhood. **MacArthur Park**, its centerpiece, is prone to drug related violence, but has been restored and enhanced with art works.

8 McManus & Morgan Handmade papers from about 20 different countries. 2506 W. 7th St. 213 387 4433

9 Charles Croze Studio (1948, H. H. Harris) Superbly landscaped plot and a daringly cantilevered balcony. 2340 W. 3rd St.

10 Granada Building (1927, Franklin Harper) Picturesque Spanish-inspired complex of offices and studios, walkways, and patios. 672 S. Lafayette Park Pl.

11 Shriners Hospital for Crippled Children Replacement Facility/Expansion (1985, BTA) Two story multipurpose rooms and rooftop terrace atop a brick podium. The interiors are open, light, and airy. 3160 Geneva St, between Virgil & Commonwealth Aves.

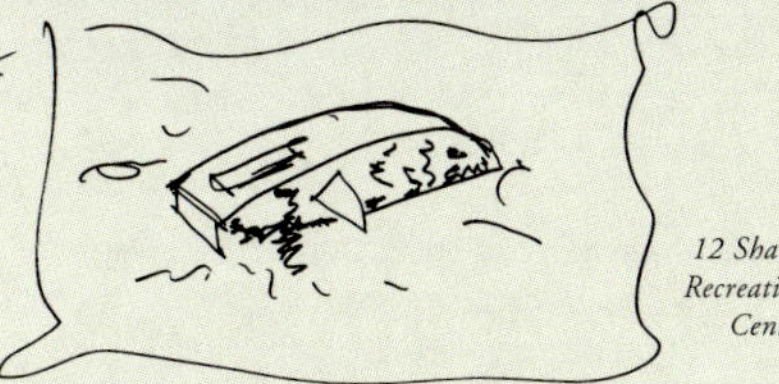

12 Shatto Recreation Center

12 Shatto Recreation Center (1992, Steven Ehrlich) Tough but elegant concrete block shell, inspired by the form of a whale, with a triangular entrance canopy as its dorsal fin. Abstract wall relief by Ed Moses. 3191 W. 4th St, near Vermont Ave.

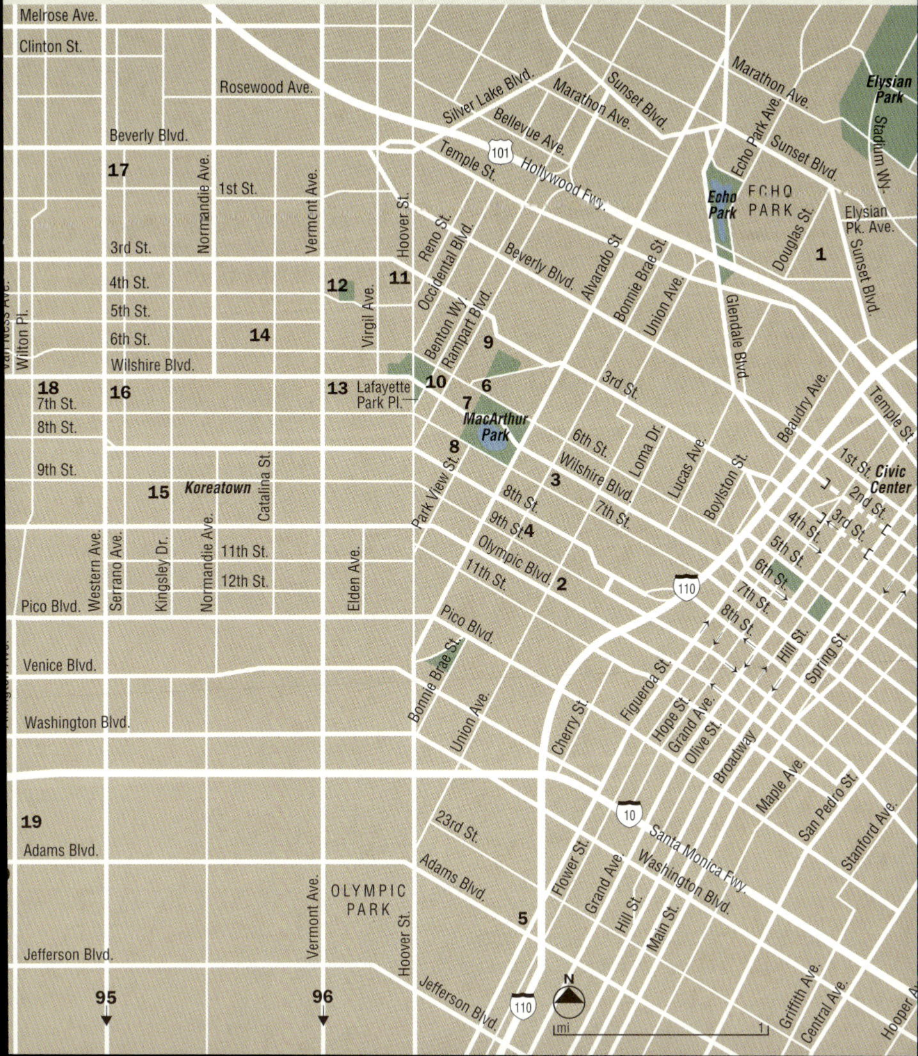

13 **Southwestern University School of Law Library** (1928, John & Donald Parkinson; restored & remodeled 1997, Altoon & Porter) The former Bullocks Wilshire is a heroic zig zag moderne landmark, a cathedral of commerce—and one of the first department stores to be designed for the convenience of motorists, with a porte cochere facing back over a parking lot. Sensitively renovated and creatively adapted to play a new role. Occasional tours during summer vacation. New Gatehouse (1999, Richard Corsini) comprises a lantern-like security kiosk, a perimeter wall, and landscaping in the SE corner of the site. 3050 Wilshire Blvd. 213 738 6825

14 **Chapman Shopping Center** (1929, Morgan, Walls & Clements; restored 1988, Levin & Associates) Stores open onto an auto court behind the Churrigueresque street facade. 3465 W. 6th St.

15 **Harvard Apts** (1992, Kanner Architects) Ham and Swiss on white to go: whimsy enlivens this low cost, stucco apartment block with its porthole windows. 901 S. Harvard Blvd. The same firm did a striking, low cost facade for existing apartments nearby at 686 S. St. Andrews Pl.

16 **Wiltern Center** (1931, Morgan, Walls & Clements; theater by G. Albert Landsburg, murals by Anthony B. Heinsbergen; restored 1985, Levin & Associates) Landmark zig zag moderne tower with two story wings clad in green terracotta. Beyond the sunburst corner canopy is a brilliantly planned, gorgeously decorated, movie palace turned performing arts center. Wilshire Blvd. at Western Ave. 323 380 5005 or 323 380 5030. Located in one wing is:

16 **Atlas Bar & Grill** (1989, Ron Meyers) Fanciful decor and live entertainment. A hip, late night crowd and OK food. 3760 Wilshire Blvd. 213 380 8400

17 **KFC** (1991, Grinstein/Daniels) Fast food in a Constructivist pavilion commissioned by an art loving franchisee. 340 N. Western Ave.

18 **Korean Youth Center** (1993, Hak Sik Son) Low income housing atop ground floor offices and community spaces on a long, skinny site.

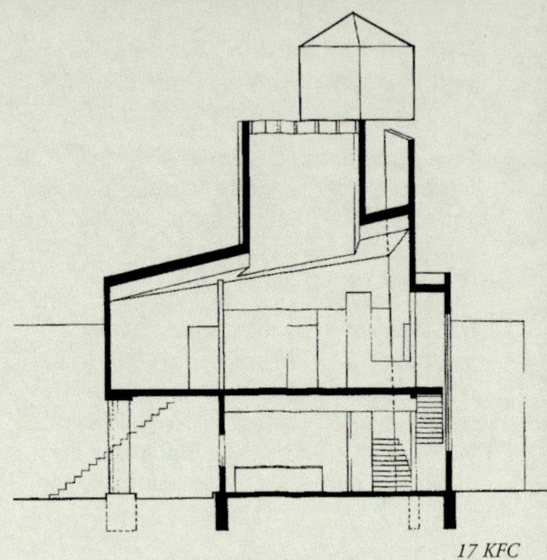

17 KFC

Apartments and lofts are set at an angle to the street to pull in light and views, and to break up the facades. 680 S. Wilton Pl. Son employed a similar strategy on his new classroom block for the **Wilton Place Elementary School**, a block south, creating a neighborhood scale and rhythm in the expansive facade.

19 **William Andrews Clark Memorial Library North Range** (1990, Barton Phelps & Associates) Extendable linear range, containing book storage, offices, and meeting rooms, which transforms a private library into UCLA's study center for 17th and 18th century English literature. The new block plays off the red brick perimeter wall, and complements the handsome baroque revival library (1926, Robert Farquhar). 2520 Cimarron St. 323 731 8529

20 **Fitzgerald House** (1903, J. C. Newsom) Another wonderfully inventive variation on Queen Anne, nicely restored. 3115 W. Adams Blvd.

Larchmont Village Two blocks of classy shops, interspersed with hardware, cafes, and other standbys, extends from 1st St. to Beverly Blvd. A community treasure accessible to all.

21 **Hollyhock** English and French 17th to 19th century furniture and objects, plus William Yeoward crystal. 214 N. Larchmont Blvd. 323 931 3400

16 Wiltern Theater

Black: exterior only, or open to public **Blue:** interior; by appt. only **Red:** private residence, do not disturb **Green:** park, or public open space

22 Girasole Tiny neighborhood north Italian trattoria. 225½ N. Larchmont Blvd. 323 464 6978

23 Dawson's Books Specializes in printing, photography and western Americana. 535 N. Larchmont Blvd. 323 469 2186

24 House (1929-30, J. C. Smale) Zig zag moderne cube; a standout among the Tudor and Spanish houses of Hancock Park, LA's pre-eminent old money neighborhood that's now drawing in discerning new buyers and is worth exploring just for the width of the streets and the beauty of the landscaping. 191 Hudson Ave. at 2nd St.

25 Campanile (1989, Schweitzer BIM) Gutsy, award-winning cuisine in an inventive remodel of a Spanish style building. Next door is the superb **La Brea Bakery**. 624 S. La Brea Ave. 323 938 1447

Feininger, and other legendary photojournalists. 332 ½ N. La Brea Ave. 323 634 7887

30 La Brea Antique Collection Time capsule of '50s Americana, juxtaposed with furniture and artifacts from earlier decades. 334 N. La Brea Ave. 323 938 9444

31 Outside Vintage patio furniture. 442 N. La Brea Ave. 323 934 1254

32 Retro Gallery Glass of the '40s and '50s from Scandinavia, Murano and Blanko in West Virginia. 524 ½ N. La Brea Ave. 323 936 5261

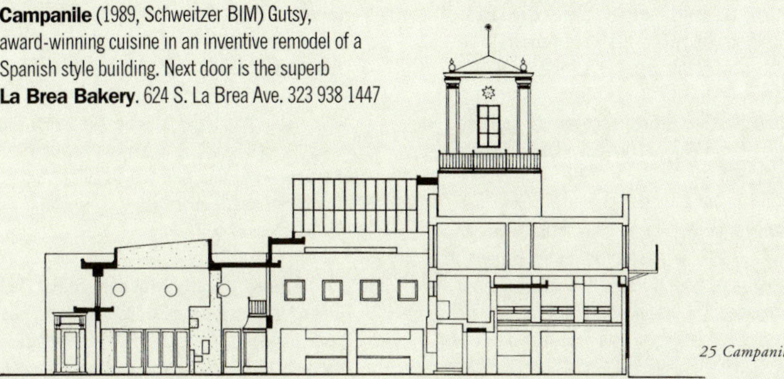

25 Campanile

26 Diamond Fabric Vast array of bargains and remnants; a favorite source for cost-conscious decorators. 611 S. La Brea Ave. 323 931 8148

27 Liz's Antique Hardware A century of door furniture, light fittings, and decorative accessories. 435 S. La Brea Ave. 323 939 4403

28 Silk Trading Co. Raw silk, velvets, damasks and mohair, plus tassels and trim. 360 S. La Brea Ave. at 4th. 323 954 9280

28 AZ Productions (1998, Studio 0.10) Purist geometry washed by overhead light within a bow-truss warehouse for a post production sound studio. 340 S. La Brea Ave. 323 934 1321

29 Paul Kopeikin Vintage and contemporary photography by Eugene Meatyard, Jock Sturges, Robert Lyons, and others. 138 N. La Brea Ave. 323 937 0765

29 Fahey-Klein Vintage and contemporary photography, especially fashion and documentary. 148 N. La Brea Ave. 323 934 2250

29 Fat Chance Furnishings of the '40s and '50s. 162 N. La Brea Ave. 323 930 1960

29 Jan Kesner Richard Misrach, John Humble, and Rob Casey are among the 30 modern and contemporary photographers whose work can be seen here. 164 N. La Brea Ave. 323 938 6834

30 Apex Fine Art David Barenholtz shows work by Alfred Eisenstaedt, Margaret Bourke-White, Andreas

33 Area Bill Wilson's FreWil Studio puts a contemporary spin on mid-century modern furnishings. 605 N. La Brea Ave. 323 934 8474

34 Skank World offers its eclectic treasures in what looks like a Goodwill outlet. Open Tu-Sa, 2:15-6pm only. 7205 Beverly Blvd. 323 939 7858

35 kbond (2000, Jansen & Goldstein) Installation artist Karen Kimmel and partner James Bond moved from New York to establish this luminous men's clothing boutique with its separate zones for sports, classic, and innovative wear. 7257 Beverly Blvd. 323 939 9779

36 Insomnia One of a cluster of bohemian coffee houses. Shady sidewalk tables, funky interior with plush sofas; art on the walls, rock from the speakers. Open till late. 7286 Beverly Blvd. 323 931 4943. Shares a streamline corner building with fashion star **Tyler Trafficante** who will be happy to dress you for a starring role on the Oscar telecast. Mere mortals are free to drool. 323 931 9678

37 Brenda Antin Antique and reproduction British colonial furnishings, plus provocative oddities. 7319 Beverly Blvd. 323 934 8451

38 Stephen Cohen Contemporary European and vintage modern photography. 7358 Beverly Blvd. 323 937 5525

38 Modernica Skillful reproductions of Eames, Weber, and other mid-century masters, plus a few originals. 7368 Beverly Blvd. 323 933 0383

38 In House Interiors Spare, stylish showroom for sculptural wood and upholstered furniture by Mark Zuckerman and Montgomery Lawton. 7370 Beverly Blvd. 323 931 4420

38 Richard Telles Gallery Large sculpture and installations by up-and-coming LA artists. 7380 Beverly Blvd. 323 965 5578

39 A. J. Heinsbergen (1925, Claude Beelman & A. B. Heinsbergen) Courtyard office block, disguised as a doll-scale moated chateau. 7415 Beverly Blvd.

40 Warisan Indonesian and Chinese antiques and contemporary crafts—especially teak furniture and lighting from Bali, where this store made its reputation. 7470 Beverly Blvd. 323 938 3960

41 Design Hardware Sophisticated door furniture and plumbing fixtures at bargain prices. 6053 3rd St. 323 930 1330

Miracle Mile Tattered relics of its moderne heyday survive amid the new developments and parking lots along Wilshire, from Highland Ave. West to Fairfax Ave. Standouts include # 5209 (1929, Morgan, Walls & Clements), a black and gold miniature of their long razed Richfield tower downtown; # 5217 (1930, Meyer & Holler), a set-back corner tower; **Dominguez-Wilshire Building,** # 5410 (1930, Morgan, Walls & Clements); **El Rey** movie house, # 5519 (1936, W. Clifford Balch).

42 La Boca (2000, Ron Meyers) Eric Basualto's nuevo Latino restaurant is housed in the landmark **Dark Room** (1935, Marcus Miller). Meyers also designed the **Conga Room & Cafe** next door. 5370 Wilshire Blvd. 323 938 1696

43 Desmond's (1929, Gilbert S. Underwood) A fine zig zag tower. On the ground floor is **Ace Contemporary Exhibitions** showing work in different media by emerging and established artists, including Tim Hawkinson and Jannis Kounellis. 5514 Wilshire Blvd. 323 935 4411

45 Wilshire Courtyard (1987, McLarend, Vasquez & Partners) Polished low-rise commercial development. Two stepped-back U plan blocks, set at an angle to the street and faced in brown granite, enclose a paved courtyard with slate obelisks. 5700 & 5750 Wilshire Blvd. **Goethe House** presents lectures, concerts and movies from Germany. 323 525 3388

46 Craft & Folk Art Museum (1994, Hodgetts + Fung) Inventive remodel of two nondescript buildings, with a new structure occupying the space between. Lively changing exhibitions of crafts from around the world. 5800 Wilshire Blvd. 323 937 4230

47 George C. Page Museum of La Brea Discovery (1976, Thornton & Fagan Associates) Space frame and grassy berms enclose a display of finds from the neighboring tar pits. Don't miss the heart-wrenching fiberglass sculpture (visible from Wilshire) of a mastodon sinking into the ooze as its family grieves. 5801 Wilshire Blvd. 323 934 7243

47 Hancock Park (1999, Olin Partnership with Fong Hart Schneider Partners) The area between Page and LACMA and around the tar pits has been landscaped as a public retreat, with signage by Sussman-Prejza, and a restroom by Syndesis which is quite the best of its kind since Piers Gough's landmark structure in West London. All this, plus site-specific art works and an amphitheater make for a thrilling Sunday in the Park with (or without) George.

48 Los Angeles County Museum of Art (1964, Pereira Associates; extended 1986, Hardy Holzman Pfeiffer Associates; renovated 2000, Kirkpatrick Associates) The three original pavilions have been stitched together and concealed from the street by the Robert O. Anderson Building, a limestone, green terra-cotta and glass brick wedge with a huge portal which pays homage to the streamline moderne Coulter's Store, a vanished highlight of Miracle Mile. Its galleries house major exhibitions and the 20th century art collection—just part of LACMA's rich holdings of Western, Asian, and decorative arts. Steps lead up, past a sculpture garden, to an enclosed plaza. The **Pentimento Cafe** (323 857 4761) is operated by Joachuim Splichal. The **Cafeteria** (2000, Belzberg Architects) has been upgraded. Excellent book and gift store, and cafe. Art movies, lectures and avant-garde music are presented in the Bing Auditorium.

48 Los Angeles County Museum of Art

Beyond the sculpture garden is the **Japanese Pavilion** (1988, Bruce Goff & Bart Prince), a last, wild fling by the Oklahoma maverick and his talented protege. The curved beams that support the roof are inspired by Japan; the fieldstone and green stucco walls are pure '50s. Edo era scrolls and screens from the Joe D. Price Collection are displayed in niches and viewed from descending ramps; other Japanese masterworks are displayed in the west gallery. 5905 Wilshire Blvd. 323 857 6111

49 LACMA West/Former May Company (1940, A. C. Martin & S. A. Marx; remodeled 1998, Kirkpatrick Associates) Brilliant adaptation of a landmark department store, with its black framed, gold mosaic cylinder anchoring the corner. Temporary exhibition spaces are juxtaposed with the Boone Children's Gallery. Sharing the ground floor is the **Southwest Museum Satellite** (1998, Chris Carradine with Gruen Associates). The chief concept architect of Walt Disney Imagineering has transformed a claustrophobic interior into a subtle evocation of the Southwest as a setting for the parent museum's priceless collection of Native American artifacts. Wilshire Blvd. at Fairfax Ave. 323 221 2164

50 Petersen Automotive Museum Housed in an ugly department store made more unsightly by the addition of fins, and facade promotion of the kind one would expect from the publisher of *Hot Rod* and *Guns & Ammo*. Occasional exhibitions of Duesenbergs and other classic cars, plus lowriders and pop stuff. 6060 Wilshire Blvd. 323 964 6356

51 6150 Wilshire Blvd. An unremarkable building converted to house some notable galleries. They include:

Domestic Seattle-based designer Roy McMakin furnished the Getty Center offices and several houses with his quirky furniture made from fallen timbers, examples of which are shown here. 323 936 8206

Acme Paintings, sculpture, and photography by such artists as Uta Barth, Miles Coolidge, and Kurt Kauper. 323 857 5942

Marc Foxx International contemporary art by Olafur Eliasson, Frances Stark, Hiroshi Sugito, and others. 323 857 5571

Works on Paper (1999, Richard Corsini) Intimacy, color, and the manipulation of natural light are key features of a showcase for drawings by Franz Ackerman, Jeremy Blake, and Elizabeth Bryant. 323 964 9675

Karyn Lovegrove Conceptual art by Ingrid Calame and Simon Periton is a specialty of this new gallery. 323 525 1755

52 Buck House (1934, R. M. Schindler) Marvelous composition of floating planes that presents a private face to the street and opens up to the garden. 8th St. at Genesee Ave.

53 Mackey Apartments (1939, R. M. Schindler; restored 1995, Central Office of Architecture) The Austrian government bought this four unit block as a residence for visiting artists and architects (see MAK Center, p 33). It demonstrates how much can be achieved with a few interlocking stucco volumes. 1137 S. Cochran Ave. Open for exhibitions and by appointment. 323 651 1510

54 Dunsmuir Apartments (1937, Gregory Ain) International Style classic. Four two-story units perform an elegant side step up a gentle slope. The north (entrance) side is clerestory-lit; the south opens to private yards and terraces. 1261 S. Dunsmuir Ave.

55 Park La Brea High- and low-rise '40s apartments, grouped to create a 176 acre garden community— a scaled down version of Le Corbusier's *Ville Radieuse*. 3rd to 6th St, Cochran St. to Fairfax Ave.

56 Samy's Camera Tops for film, processing, and accessories; also to rent or buy equipment at competitive prices. 431 S. Fairfax Ave. 323 938 2420

57 407 Architect/designer Leslie Shapiro joined forces with cabinetmaker James Matranga to create deceptively plain, solid wood furniture and cabinetry. 407 S. Fairfax Ave. 323 525 1718

58 Farmers Market Touristy but irresistible for its shady food stands and appetizing displays. Begun as a Depression era co-op. Good bets for eating include **The Gumbo Pot** (323 933 0358) and **Kokomo Cafe** (323 933 0773). 3rd St. at Fairfax Ave.

59 Sonrisa Burke and Peggy Byrnes search out vintage American metal furniture. 7609 Beverly Blvd. 323 935 8438

60 CBS Television City (1952, Pereira & Luckman; additions 1976, Gin Wong Associates) Studios and offices housed in hi-tech boxes. 7800 Beverly Blvd.

61 Empirica Gallery Wannabe Dr. Frankensteins and hard-to-please decorators should snap up these "Artifacts of Science, Technology and the Industrial Revolution—for Home or Lab." 7916 Beverly Blvd. 323 634 7323

61 Shelter Elegant accessories, including some of the best looking bowls in town; simple furniture, bed linens. 7920 Beverly Blvd. 323 937 3222

61 Modern One Owner Ben Storck draws collectors with his chic treasures by William Haines, Robsjohn-Gibbings, Vladimir Kagan, and other mid-century stars. 7956 Beverly Blvd. 323 651 5082

62 Mimosa Authentic French bistro fare in a room that is a model of unpretentious charm, plus a sidewalk terrace. 8009 Beverly Blvd. 323 655 8895

63 LA Modern Auctions Peter & Shannon Loughrey are LA's best source for vintage modern furniture, auctioning bargains and high priced rarities every month. There's a major catalogue sale three times a year. 8057 Beverly Blvd. 323 904 1950

63 Twentieth Stefan Lawrence's quirky selection of vintage modern furniture by designers you haven't heard of. 8057 Beverly Blvd. 323 904 1200

64 Salick Offices (1991-95, Morphosis) Bold remodels of generic office towers for a company that operates cancer clinics. 8150 & 8201 Beverly Blvd. The **Comprehensive Cancer Center** (1988, Morphosis) at Cedars Sinai Medical Center is closed to the public.

65 Pane e Vino Fine Italian food in a charming patio and dining room that resonate with industry buzz. 8265 Beverly Blvd. 323 651 4600

66 Healing Waters (1993, Regina Pizzinini/Leon Luxemburg) Luminous, top-lit storefront; a serene white setting for colored oils and essences. 136 S. Orlando Ave. at Beverly Blvd. 323 651 4656

67 International Silks & Woolens Fine fabrics imported from France and Italy. 8347 Beverly Blvd. 323 653 6453

68 Ubon Handsome, moderately priced offshoot of Matsuhisa, specializing in noodle dishes. 8530 Beverly Blvd. 310 854 1115

69 Tail-o'-the-Pup (1938, Milton J. Black) Signature hot dog stand—an LA pop classic. 329 San Vicente Blvd. 310 652 4517

70 Michael Rudin French, British and Dutch colonial pieces, alongside custom furniture and lighting wrought in iron. 8132 W. 3rd St. 323 658 7601

71 OK Lawrence Schaffer showcases Noguchi lamps, ceramics, glass, and other craft objects by talented young artisans. 8303 W. 3rd St. 323 653 3501

72 Zipper Pop and serious design objects and books. 8316 W. 3rd St. 323 951 0620

73 Freehand Well-crafted gifts and occasional exhibitions of designs from Europe and the US. 8413 W. 3rd St. 323 685 2607

74 Sushi Roku Terminally trendy crowd flocks to this serious Japanese restaurant with decor that evokes a zen garden in Kyoto. 8445 W. 3rd St. 323 655 6767

75 Katsu 3rd Pacific New Wave food in a minimalist room. 8636 W. 3rd St. 310 273 3605

76 Chaya Brasserie (1984, Grinstein/Daniels) Japanese serenity combined with the informality of a Parisian brasserie. 8741 Alden Dr. 310 859 8833

77 Japanache Japanese antiques, including tansu chests, scrolls, and ceramic vases. 146 N. Robertson Blvd. 310 657 0155

78 Cynthia Leight Opticians (1999, Space International) 20 different leading brands are displayed to best advantage in a cool space. 123 S. Robertson Blvd. 310 858 7399

78 Bulthaup Kitchens If you can appreciate (and afford) the perfection of a Rolls Royce, this is the place to find your dream kitchen. 153 S. Robertson Blvd. 310 288 3875

79 Modern Living No need to go to Milan: a carefully edited selection of the best new furnishings by Cassina, Capellino and B&B, plus witty housewares from Alessi are conveniently close. 8775 Beverly Blvd. 323 657 8775

80 Diva High style contemporary European furniture and lighting—including the best of Ingo Maurer. 8801 Beverly Blvd. 310 278 3191. Next door is **Fontana d'Arte**, a venerable Italian manufacturer of lighting and art glass. 8807 Beverly Blvd. 310 247 9933

80 Jules Seltzer/Herman Miller for the Home Top office furniture and classics by Eames, Nelson, and Bertoia for home offices and architects' homes. 8833 Beverly Blvd. 310 274 7233

80 Linea Stylish furniture, lighting, and glass by European architects and sculptors. 8843 Beverly Blvd. 310 273 5425

81 SEE Goodman-Charlton have moved to New York, and the contemporary furniture store they established in the former Herman Miller showroom (designed by the Eames Office) now features work by Karim Rashid, Ron Arad, Patrick Chia, and Peter Miele. 8806 Beverly Blvd. 310 385 1919

81 Dialogica Geometric relief rugs, romantic sofas, and elegant cabinetry are standouts. 8820 Beverly Blvd. 310 888 0008

82 Lief Empire, Biedermeier, and contemporary European furniture and accessories. 8922 Beverly Blvd. 310 550 8118

83 Palazzetti Reproductions of classic 20th century furniture & rugs, plus new designs by Poltronova, Frigerio, Parobell, and Europa lighting. 9008 Beverly Blvd. 310 273 2225

Black: exterior only, or open to public   **Blue:** interior; by appt. only   **Red:** private residence, do not disturb   **Green:** park, or public open space

84 Natalee Thai (1998, Coscia Day) Folded planes of maple ply animate a dumb storefront, disguise a jutting elevator, and pull you into the space. The architects borrowed from fractal geometry and chaos theory—but it won't stop you from enjoying the mee krob and spicy shrimp. 998 S. Robertson Blvd. at Olympic Blvd. 310 855 9380

84 Electric Sun (1999, Escher GuneWardena) Tanning parlor of rare refinement with an interior of intersecting planes and space manipulated by light. 998 S. Robertson Blvd. 310 659 8301

85 Pearl Great choice and value in art supplies. 1250 S. La Cienega Blvd. 310 854 4900

86 Robertson Branch Library (1997, Steven Ehrlich) A split copper-clad boat form serves as a marquee for this impressive structure, which is lofted above ground level parking on a busy commercial strip. The goal is to draw users in and provide them with a welcoming, well-lit place to read. 1719 S. Robertson Blvd. 310 840 2147

87 Helm's Bakery Building (1930, E. L. Bruner) Stately PWA moderne industrial building, recycled as ground floor retail and upstairs offices for inventive companies. These include colorful, sophisticated conversions of raw space (1991-95, Alison Wright) for the **Rabuck Agency** (310 815 8225), **Johans & Sons Advertising** (310 559 1041), and **Industrial Creative** (310 559 9661). 8800 Venice Blvd. Management: 310 204 1865

88 St. Elmo's Village (Roderick Sykes; restored 1994, Alex Istanbullu & John Kaliski) An artists' community set within a complex of 10 '20s bungalows, set off by painted paving of Caribbean color and exuberance. Visitors are welcome. 4830 St. Elmo Dr, off La Brea Ave, between Venice & Washington Blvds.

South of Midtown

89 Pann's (1955, Armet & Davis) Googie style at its most demented; a glass-walled coffee shop with exotic greenery and an eccentrically angled roof. La Tijera, La Cienega & Centinela Blvd.

90 Randy's Donuts (1954) Pop icon of a giant donut. 805 W. Manchester Ave. at La Cienega Blvd, Inglewood.

91 Stanford M. Anderson Water Treatment Plant (1977, Kahn, Kappe, Lotery, Boccato) Steel and glass box that reveals the equipment, and a colorful graphic to explain how it operates. SW corner of Eucalyptus & Beach Aves.

92 Baldwin Hills Village (1940-41, Reginald Johnson, Wilson & Merrill, Robert E. Alexander; Clarence S. Stein consultant & site planner) Rare instance of affordable housing that almost everyone covets. Two story, stucco houses and terraces are ranged along shady pedestrian paths and greens. The formerly barren 80 acre site is now full of mature trees. 5300 Rodeo Rd, between La Cienega Blvd. & La Brea Ave.

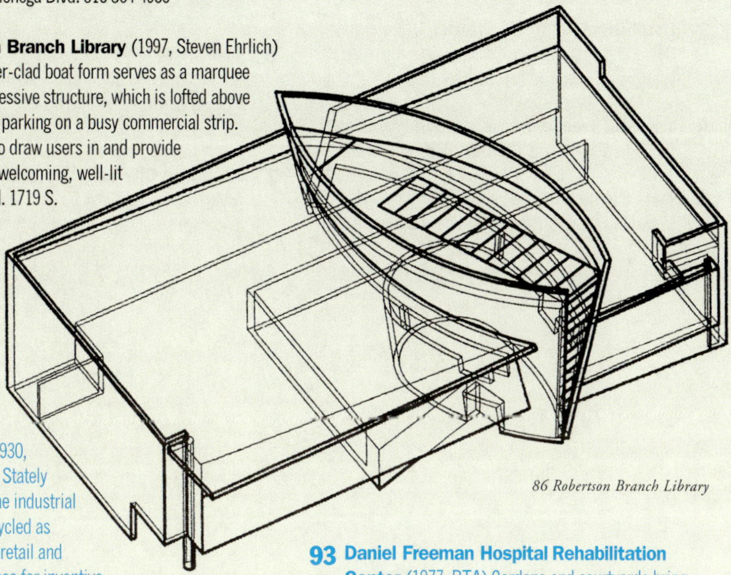

86 Robertson Branch Library

93 Daniel Freeman Hospital Rehabilitation Center (1977, BTA) Gardens and courtyards bring natural light to every part of this three story building, making it easy to find one's way. Innovative design that cares for its users. 333 N. Prairie Ave, Inglewood. 310 674 7050

94 Academy Theater (1939, S. Charles Lee) The finest of Lee's prolific output of streamline moderne movie theaters has a spiral-finned tower. Now used as a church. 3100 Manchester Blvd. at Crenshaw Blvd.

95 Antique Stove Heaven Sales and repairs of classic stoves, especially O'Keefe & Merritt. 5414 S. Western Ave. 213 298 5581

96 Vermont Village Plaza (1997, Daniel Solomon) Competition-winning urban revitalization scheme, sponsored by First Interstate Bank in an area still scarred by the 1989 riots. It interweaves affordable housing and new businesses, and redefines the street. Vermont Ave. at 81st St.

Around the turn of the century, affluent Easterners wintered here in resort hotels and commissioned Craftsman bungalows. Despite the intrusion of freeways, crass commercial blocks and summer smog, Pasadena remains the grande dame of the region, full of handsome streets and architectural treasures, trees and mountain views; also, a revitalized **Old Town** with lively stores and restaurants.

1 **Pasadena Railroad Station** (1935, H. L. Gilman) Beguiling Spanish Colonial depot, the preferred stop for celebrities leaving or arriving on the Super Chief before Union Station was built. 222 Raymond Ave. Best seen from Arroyo Pkwy, across the tracks.

2 **Hotel Green** (1898-1903, Frederick L. Roehrig) Overpoweringly ornate resort hotel, now converted to apartments. Raymond Ave. at Green St.

3 **The Folk Tree** Latin American folk art, textiles and furniture. 199 & 217 S. Fair Oaks Dr. 626 793 4828

4 **Twin Palms** Hearty bistro food at bargain prices served in a cavernous barn or a tented courtyard, with palms to confirm you are still in southern California. 101 W. Green St. 626 577 2567

5 **Mendenhall Gallery** Strong emphasis on narrative and fantasy, including Ray Turner's romantic landscapes and the surrealist paintings of Mark Ryden. 41 N. Fair Oaks Ave. 626 792 0162

6 **Yujean Kang's** High praise for pricey new Chinese cuisine, served in a spare, elegant room. 67 N. Raymond Ave. 626 585 0855

6 **Xiomara/Oye!** A fresh spin for Latino cuisine in front, and an Asian touch for Cuban cooking in back, plus a setting of restrained elegance. 69 N. Raymond Ave. 626 796 2520

6 **Café Bizou** Modest prices and consistent quality draw enthusiastic crowds to this new branch of the hottest French bistro in the Valley. 91 N. Raymond Ave. 626 792 9923

7 **Pasadena City Hall** (1925-27, John Blakewell/ Arthur Brown, Jr.) Gutsy baroque tower with landscaped fountain court by the architects of

San Francisco's City Hall. It's the centerpiece of a half-realized Beaux Arts civic center that includes the Renaissance-style post office and public library. Garfield at Holly St.

8 **Police Facility** (1990, Robert A. M. Stern) Bravura historicism, with tall arches, overscaled volutes, and an attic story; a fine companion for City Hall and the **Florentine Renaissance Gas Company** (1929) next door. 1207 N. Garfield Ave.

9 **Plaza Las Fuentes** (1989-92, Moore Ruble Yudell; landscaping by Lawrence Halprin) Fountains, tilework, and plantings enliven a sequence of pedestrian spaces linking a hotel and mixed-use complex E. of City Hall. Bounded by Colorado Blvd. & Walnut, Euclid & Los Robles Aves.

10 **Pacific Asia Museum** (1924, Marston, Van Pelt & Maybury) Spanish Revival courtyard building in Chinese fancy dress which hosts remarkable exhibitions of East Asian art in addition to its permanent collection. 46 N. Los Robles Ave. 626 449 2742

11 **Norton Simon Museum** (1969, Ladd & Kelsey; remodeled 1996-99, Frank O. Gehry & Associates) One of America's great collections of European masters, East Indian and Southeast Asian art, and one of the city's best museum shops were housed in a bunker with rounded corners and an incoherent plan. This has now been transformed into a cool, serene sequence of handsomely proportioned, light filled galleries, enriched with dignified materials and colors. Sculpture is displayed in grounds relandscaped by Nancy Goslee Power. 411 W. Colorado Blvd. 626 449 6840

12 **Colorado Street Bridge** (1913, John Drake Mercereau) Pasadena's reinforced concrete Pont du Gard, newly equipped with steel fences to deter potential suicides. Colorado Blvd. at Arroyo Seco.

13 **Prospect Boulevard** Stone entrance piers by Greene & Greene and mature camphor trees make this one of the city's most desirable streets. Prospect Crescent leads to **La Miniatura** (#645; 1923, Frank Lloyd Wright; studio, 1926, Lloyd Wright), the first and best of FLW's concrete block houses. It can be glimpsed from below on Rosemont Ave.

14 Gamble House

14 Gamble House (1908, Charles & Henry Greene) Polished teak, original furnishings, and Tiffany glass make this superbly maintained Craftsman interior a must see. Happy is the visiting architect who gets to stay here as a guest of the USC School of Architecture. One hour tours Th-Su, noon-3pm. Well-stocked bookstore. 4 Westmoreland Pl. 626 793 3334. Next door is the **Cole House** (1906, Greene & Greene), now church offices, with its magnificent stone chimney.

14 Duncan-Irwin House (1900-1906, Greene & Greene) Craftsman gem, superbly sited and beautifully composed. 240 N. Grand Ave. Around the corner, looking north to the mountains, is **Arroyo Terrace**, lined with less visible Greene & Greene bungalows.

15 Kubly House (1964, Craig Ellwood) Mies goes to Japan in this woodsy post-and-beam structure. 215 La Vereda Rd.

16 Dumbacher House (1996, Hagy Belzberg) Shoehorned onto a steep, wedge-shaped site is a house that epitomizes southern California living at its best. Space flows through the main floor living areas from sunken patio to sharp tipped prow—a balcony overlooking the valley and Rose Bowl; bedrooms and garage are tucked into the hillside below. 1234 Linda Ridge Rd, off Linda Vista Ave.

17 Art Center College of Design (1976, Craig Ellwood) Miesian steel-framed glass box that spans a ravine and neatly bundles together the activities of this prestigious school of fine and applied arts. Opening off the reception area is the skylit **Alyce de Roulet Williamson Gallery** (1992, Frederick Fisher), a box within a box. The latest addition is the **Garden Pavilion** (2000, Hodgetts + Fung), an airy gathering/ exhibition space for students. Under the leadership of Art Center's new director, Richard Koshalek, Frank O. Gehry & Associates are developing a master plan for expansion; if realized, the Portuguese architect Alvaro Siza would play a leading role. Gallery open Tu-Su, noon-5pm; Th til 9pm. 1700 Lida St. 626 584 5000

18 Jamie House (2000, Escher GuneWardena) Two concrete piers loft an 84 ft. long steel-framed, board-clad structure above a precipitous slope to maximize views and minimize its impact on the land; a garage separates the adult and family zones. 1472 Inverness Dr.

19 Condominiums (1982, Batey & Mack) White stucco courtyard complex, Cycladic in its purity, but sharp edged. 371-79 W. Bellevue Dr.

19 Apartment Court (1926, Robert H. Ainsworth) Traditional garden court at its best: low, Andalusian-style buildings, flowering trees, central fountain. 339-53 W. California Blvd.

20 Bruce Graney Refined English and French 18th and 19th century country furniture and antiques. 1 W. California Blvd. 626 449 9547

21 Sonnies Folk art and clothing for women and children from India, China, and Indonesia. 1007 S. Fair Oaks Ave. 626 799 8764

22 Mission Tile West European and American tiles, from 150 makers can be ordered. 853 Mission St. 626 799 4595

23 Miltimore House (1911, Irving Gill) Astonishingly forward looking for its date and location, demonstrating how Gill anticipated European modernism in his stripped down reinterpretation of the Mission aesthetic. 1301 Chelten Way.

24 Peter Lai Dressmaker extraordinaire, patronized by ladies who want to make a grand entrance in silks and satins, impeccably cut. 2571 Mission St, San Marino. 626 799 4645

25 Experimental Dome House (1946, Wallace Neff) A historicist with a conscience, Neff built several of these prototypes for a low cost house, and lived here in the late '70s. This may be the last surviving example in the US, though others were built in Africa. Gunnite was sprayed onto reinforcing rods that were supported from within by a balloon. 1097 S. Los Robles Ave.

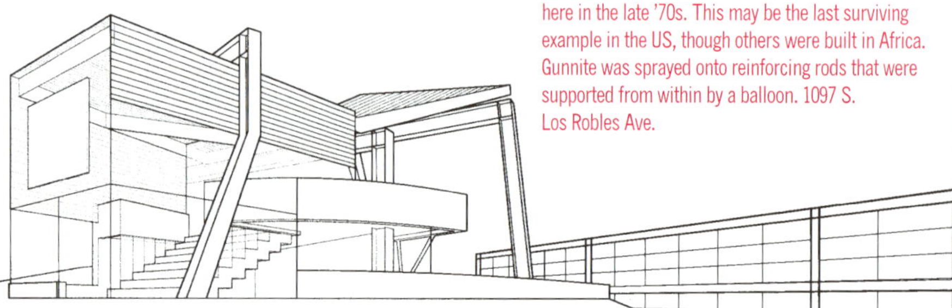

17 Art Center College of Design Garden Pavillion

Black: exterior only, or open to public **Blue:** interior; by appt. only **Red:** private residence, do not disturb **Green:** park, or public open space

26 Pasadena Playhouse (1925, Elmer Grey) Flourishing theater leads out of a charming courtyard. 37 S. El Molino Ave. 626 356 7529

27 Warner Building (1927, Jess Stanton) Newly refurbished zig zag moderne commercial building with exuberant terracotta frieze; the best of several Art Deco facades along this commercial artery. 481 E. Colorado Blvd.

28 Vroman's Books A local institution with a large, well-chosen stock. 695 E. Colorado Blvd. at Oak Knoll Ave. 626 449 5320. Close by is **Vroman's Museum Books**, a specialized offshoot of the main store. 340 S. Lake Blvd. 626 396 1670

29 Pashgian Bros. Exceptional Oriental carpets and repairs. 993 E. Colorado Blvd. 626 796 7888

30 Bullock's Pasadena (1947, Wurdeman & Becket) Elegant late streamline department store (now Macy's) set back behind Ruth Shelhorne's landscaping. 401 S. Lake Ave.

31 R. R. Blacker House (1907, Greene & Greene) Sweeping eaves and a thrusting, brick-supported porte cochere. The house is aptly named; its walls are so dark that they seem to swallow the light. The interior has been superbly restored by new owners. 1177 Hillcrest Ave. at Wentworth Ave.

32 O'Brien House (1912, Arthur S. Heineman) Tight-knit tiers of arched roofs distinguish this Craftsman house. 1327 Oak Knoll Ave. at Ridge Way. Next door, at 1361 Ridge Way, is another Craftsman house with a striking facade of shingles and logs.

33 El Molino Viejo (1816) Most of LA's Mission-era buildings have been over restored; this water-powered adobe gristmill has authentic period character. 1120 Old Mill Rd.

San Marino

Railroad magnate Henry H. Huntington provided the land for this independently governed enclave, which was laid out with broad streets and large plots around his palatial estate a hundred years ago.

34 Huntington Library, Arts Collections & Botanical Gardens (1910, Myron Hunt & Elmer Grey) Superb 18th century English paintings in period rooms, a major book collection, and fabulous gardens, plus an especially good tea room in the rose garden (reservations: 626 683 8131). The **Virginia Steele Scott Gallery of American Art** (1984, Warner & Gray), inspired by John Russell Pope's neo-classicism, displays paintings and a permanent exhibit on the

Greene brothers. Another addition is **The Mary Lou and George Boone Gallery** (2000, Levin & Associates) sensitively adapted from the founder's garage. Tu-F, noon-4:30pm; Sa-Su, 10:30am-4:30pm. 1151 Oxford Rd. 626 405 2100, directions: 626 405 2274

35 Ostoff House (1924, George Washington Smith) The shadows of desert plants play off the expansive white wall to the south; around the corner, one can glimpse orange trees and red tiled roofs. 1778 Lombardy Rd. at Allen Ave.

36 Bourne House (1927, Wallace Neff) As sensuous as a reclining nude is this range of Andalusian farm buildings that hug the ground behind an expansive fenced garden. 2035 Lombardy Rd. Other period gems by Neff, Smith, Roland Coate, and their contemporaries line this and neighboring streets.

37 Avery House, California Institute of Technology (1996, Moore Ruble Yudell) Urbane residence for students and faculty in an abstracted version of the Mediterranean style that prevails on this campus. Public and private rooms are ranged around four courtyards, landscaped by Pamela Burton, and bound together with colonnaded walkways. Close by is MRY's **Engineering & Applied Sciences Library**.

38 Astro Motel (1957) The embodiment of early space-age design, recalling the vogue for tail fins and fire-spitting exhaust vents, which is astonishingly well preserved. 2818 E. Colorado Blvd. Close by, at the **Loud Ford Dealership**, is an elegant backlit pylon of the same era.

39 Queen Anne Cottage, LA State & County Arboretum (1886, Albert A. Bennett) Picture perfect, lakeside guest house commissioned as a honeymoon cottage by "Lucky" Baldwin on his Santa Anita ranch. Daily 9am-6pm. 301 N. Baldwin Ave, Arcadia.

40 Aztec Hotel (1925, Robert Stacy-Judd) A riot of decoration on a plain stucco box, and an atmospheric lobby, designed by an enthusiastic proponent of the pre-Columbian revival style. 311 W. Foothill Blvd. at Magnolia Ave, Monrovia.

41 Parson's Bungalow (1910, Arthur Heineman) Superb Craftsman bungalow transported from its original location in Pasdadena. 1605 E. Altadena Dr. at Porter Ave. A block away is Boulder Road, an intriguing period piece.

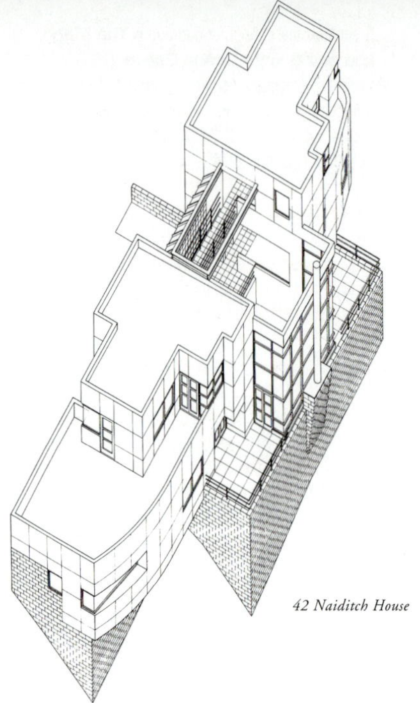

42 Naiditch House

42 Naiditch House (1994, Dean Nota) Linear sequence of rooms opening onto terraces, and stacked on the side of a ridge like a beached cruise ship. It is closed to the street but opens up to extraordinary views over mountains and wilderness, and can be best appreciated from Stonehill St. below. 3072 Zane Grey Terr, Altadena. From above the house, one can look down on Nota's bow-roofed Polyonis-Engen House (1996).

Eagle Rock/Highland Park

Midway between downtown and Pasadena, it is NW of the Pasadena Freeway (which was LA's first, completed in 1942 as the Arroyo Seco Parkway). Note the PWA moderne tunnel entry arches.

43 Southwest Museum (1912, Sumner Hunt & Silas R. Burns) Mission-style hilltop landmark containing a superb collection of Native American crafts. Special exhibitions and seasonal events. Tu-Su, 11am-5pm. 234 Museum Dr, exit Ave. 43 from freeway. 323 221 2164

43 Lummis House (1895-1910, Henry Lummis) Picturesque historicism: concrete structure faced with boulders and stucco; distressed timber beams and carvings within. F-Su, noon-4pm. 200 E. 43rd Ave. 323 222 0546

44 Occidental College (1911-38, Myron Hunt & H. C. Chambers) Decorous campus for a private university, enlivened by the sensitive remodels and additions of Levin & Associates: **Samuelson Pavilion** (1994), **Sculpture Studio** (1997), and **Johnson Studio Center** (1999). 1600 Campus Rd.

Glendale

45 Derby House (1926, Lloyd Wright) Fretted screens project from a stucco box, demonstrating the essential difference between the organic architecture of Frank Lloyd Wright and his son's use of similar elements for decorative effect. The house has been well restored and can be glimpsed from two sides. 2535 Chevy Chase Dr. at St. Andrew's Dr.

46 Forest Lawn Pious kitsch that inspired Evelyn Waugh's *The Loved One*. More fun than Disneyland for those with a well-developed sense of humor. Daily 8am-6pm. 1712 S. Glendale Ave.

47 Alex Theatre (1925, Arthur Lindley & Charles Selkirk; pylon and new facade, 1940, S. Charles Lee; remodeled 1994 for the Ratkovich Company) Glorious landmark movie palace turned performing arts center, with an enlarged stage and lobby, and a steeper rake. Behind the moderne pylon is the original Greek-Egyptian decor. 216 N. Brand Blvd.

48 Nestle USA HQ (1990, Johnson Fain Partners) Granite-faced 21 story tower, with scalloped bays contained within a five story structural grid that imparts a sculptural rhythm to the facades. 800 N. Brand Blvd.

49 European Reclamation Antique stone pavers, timbers, trusses, and handmade bricks. 4324 Brazil St. 818 241 2152

50 Brand Library (1904, Nathaniel Dryden) Inspired by the East Indian Pavilion at the 1893 Chicago World's Fair, and built by a local booster to be used as a public library and art gallery. The luxuriant grounds also contain a Queen Anne-style house that was moved here and restored. 1601 W. Mountain St. at Grandview Ave. 818 548 2051

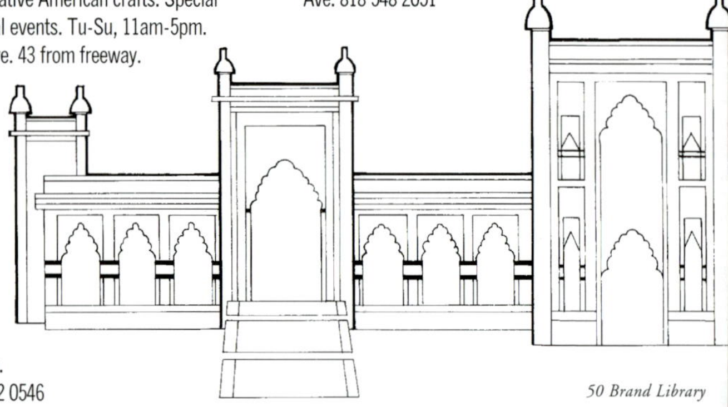

50 Brand Library

Black: exterior only, or open to public **Blue:** interior; by appt. only **Red:** private residence, do not disturb **Green:** park, or public open space

Burbank

51 **Boulder Bungalows** Fine late '20s examples of a once popular style. Olive Ave. at 9th St.

52 **Burbank City Hall** (1941, William Allen & George Lutzi) PWA moderne classic with tall, fretted screen, jazzy lobby, and fountain. Olive Ave. at 3rd St.

53 **Nickelodeon** (1997, Area) "If it looks like an office, you've failed!" said the client, and the designers met his challenge with a three-dimensional cartoon in sizzling colors to house this children's TV animation studio. 231 W. Olive Ave, Burbank. 818 736 3000

a stylized streamline train, three make-believe sound stages, and a sorcerer's hat covering the CEO's office. Brilliant interior planning—but you'll never see it; security is tighter here than at Fort Knox. The latest insertions include the **Frank G. Wells Building** (2000, Venturi Scott Brown) with a huge film reel pattern in the facade, and the **Riverside Building** (2000, Aldo Rossi), a 10 story office building. Buena Vista Dr. at Alameda Ave. 818 560 1000

55 **Warner Bros Studios** Making deals now takes precedence over making movies, and the major companies have added glitzy towers to house their Armani suited legions. At Warner Bros, you can see the '30s juxtaposition of residential-scaled

53 Nickelodeon

54 **Walt Disney Studios** (1939-40, Kem Weber; many additions) The German-born master of streamline moderne created a functional studio campus for what was then a minor company making animated shorts. Buildings, signage, and interiors are among the finest, best-preserved expressions of industrial modern in LA. Sixty years later, Disney is an 800 pound gorilla, and new structures jostle for attention. Michael Graves's overbearing red sandstone and yellow stucco **Administration Building** (1991) is crowned with a joke pediment—the Seven Dwarfs on steroids. Robert Stern's **Animation Building** (1995) is much more fun, and clearly visible from the Ventura freeway:

administration buildings and barn-like stages; across the street is a mirror glass block (1979, Charles Luckman) that houses part of the overflow. This is the only studio where you can take an authentic behind-the-scenes tour, by reservation (818 954 1744). Olive St. at Hollywood Way. Across the street is the **Warner Elektra Atlantic Building** (1981, Gibbs & Gibbs), the ultimate post-and-beam structure—a bold signature for this music company and a sun shade for the south facing offices.

Moviemakers transformed Hollywood from a farming community founded by temperate mid-Westerners into a gaudy symbol of entertainment, before moving on in search of cheaper land. Left behind was a broad strip of sound stages and workshops, flanked by modest bungalows on the flats, picturesque houses in the hills, grandiose theaters, and a treasury of period style. The long decline of this beleaguered community and tourist mecca may be finally arrested by $3 billion of new investment. Coming soon is the vast Hollywood & Highland Development (2001, Ehrenkrantz Eckstut & Kuhn) with its ersatz Babylonian arch, Premiere Theater for the Academy Awards and other spectaculars, and Marriot Renaissance Hollywood Hotel; also, a revived Cinerama Dome (2001,Gensler) and a host of smaller projects. Meanwhile, the independent city of West Hollywood tries to cope with the explosion of smart showrooms, restaurants, clubs, and traffic.

1 **Daniels House** (1993, Jeffrey Daniels) Integrally colored stucco box that stacks garage/drafting office, bedrooms, and double height living/study at the front of a steep, narrow lot to free space for a backyard. Steel fins shade expansive windows. 8617 Lookout Mountain Ave.

2 **Case Study Housing** (1994, Adele Naude Santos) Competition-winning design—sponsored by MOCA and the CRA in 1988—for 40 units of low-cost housing. Most are split-level townhouses that are entered from one of three courtyards (each with a community porch and play area) or from the garden to the south. Units are designed for through-ventilation and abundant natural light; each has a private patio. NW corner of La Brea & Franklin Aves.

3 **Yamashiro's** Old-fashioned Japanese restaurant with fabulous window views at sunset. Go for a drink and check out the 600 year old pagoda, imported in 1913 by two dealers in Asian art. 1999 N. Sycamore Ave. 323 466 5125

4 **House** (1992, Franklin D. Israel Design Associates) Partial views from the street of this striking remodel, which adds a two story sleeping pavilion and expanded living room to the trunk of a conventional bungalow, tying them together with an intense blue spinal wall. 2029 Castillian Dr. at Los Tilos Rd.

Hollywood Blvd. All but one of the ornate mansions lining the former Prospect Ave. were demolished in the '20s and '30s to create the movie colony's Main Street

and a theater district that supplanted Broadway, downtown. LA's steady shift to the west has drained its prosperity, but handsome deco and historicist facades can still be seen above the tawdry storefronts and sidewalk sleaze from La Brea Ave. to Gower St.

5 **Hollywood Roosevelt Hotel** (1927) Restored historical landmark with a retro feel. David Hockney painted the pool to the rear. 7000 Hollywood Blvd. 323 466 7000

6 **Hollywood Orangeland** (2001, RoTo Architects) A shimmering crystal by day and a glowing lantern by night: that is the promise of this faceted glass structure, wrapped with ramps leading to a rooftop terrace—all to lure tourists to Frederick's Lingerie Museum and a souvenir shop! Hollywood Blvd. at N. Orange Dr.

6 **Mann's Chinese Theatre** (1927, Meyer & Holler) Fanciful Chinese temple, a masterpiece of showmanship, with a walled forecourt that contains the world's largest autograph album. Opulent red and gold interiors. 6925 Hollywood Blvd. 323 464 8111

7 **El Capitan Theatre** (1926, Morgan, Walls & Clements; theater by G. Albert Landsburg; restored 1991 by Fields & Devereaux, J. Ronald Reed, Martin Weill & Joseph J. Musil) Behind the richly encrusted facade, riotously ornate lobbies and auditorium were stripped of '40s additions and restored to re-create a vintage movie showcase for Walt Disney pictures. 6838 Hollywood Blvd. 323 467 7674

8 **Hollywood-Highland Station** (mid 2000, Dworsky Associates) Boldly curved metal wall cladding, pulled apart to reveal the structural underpinning, abstracts the exuberance of the theaters overhead and the separate reality of the Metro tunnel. Corner of Hollywood Blvd. & Highland Ave.

9 **Highland-Camrose Bungalow Park** (1996, Levin & Associates) A new wall surrounds a leafy compound and seven early '20s clapboard bungalows that have been remodeled to serve as offices and meeting spaces for the LA Philharmonic and county employees. Nice use of color and landscaping. NW corner of Highland Ave. & Camrose Dr.

10 **The High Tower** (1920) An elevator, disguised as a campanile, and flights of steps link streamline villas on the hillside to a cul-de-sac of garages. High Tower Rd.

11 Urban Lofts (1987, Koning Eizenberg) Twin stucco towers containing stacked live/work spaces that open up to the wild hillside behind. 6947-49 Camrose Dr.

12 Hollywood Heritage Museum In 1913, Cecil B. DeMille rented this horse barn for *The Squaw Man*—the first feature-length film shot in Hollywood. It then stood at Selma and Vine, was later trucked to the Paramount lot, and moved to its present site in 1985. Restored, it exhibits mementoes of early Hollywood. Open Sa-Su, 11am-4pm; during the week in summer. 2100 N. Highland Ave. 323 874 2276

13 Hollywood Bowl LA's best cheap summer treat. A natural amphitheater, developed in the '20s as a place to enjoy music under the stars. Lloyd Wright designed the first two concert shells; Frank Gehry added acoustic spheres to a later shell in 1982. George Stanley did the moderne sculptures at the entrance, and an historical museum has been added. The LA Philharmonic and visiting artists (jazz, pop, and classical) play here, June-September. The cheap seats in back are usually available at short notice—but ticket lines are long. You can bring a picnic or get food on the grounds. Park-and-ride buses serve different parts of the city. Grounds open in summer 9am-dusk. 2301 N. Highland Ave. 323 850 2000

14 John Anson Ford Theatre (Restored 1995, Kanner Architects) Improved acoustics and access, brighter colors, and signage for this outdoor theater, built in the '30s. 2580 N. Cahuenga Blvd. off N. Vine St. 323 489 3232

15 Lake Hollywood Reservoir in an idyllic canyon. Fine view of the Hollywood sign, which was first erected in 1922 to promote the Hollywoodland subdivision, shortened in 1949 to serve as a civic advertisement, and rebuilt in 1978. The letters are 50 ft. high. To reach the lake, drive N. on Cahuenga Blvd. across Franklin Ave, right on Dix St, left on Holly Dr, sharp right on Deep Dell Pl, and left on Weidlake Dr.

16 Max Factor Building (1931, S. Charles Lee) Regency moderne shrine for the art of makeup, which may soon house a museum of Hollywood history. 1666 N. Highland Ave.

17 American Cinematheque (1922, Meyer & Holler; restored 1998, Hodgetts + Fung) Impressario Sid Grauman commissioned the Egyptian Theatre as a venue for gala movie premieres and live stage shows that preceded the screenings. The extravagance bankrupted him; the theater was torn apart by subsequent owners, but its gaudy remains have been restored. A new structure has been woven through the old to create two state of the art auditoria that present the best of world cinema most nights of the week. During the day you can see *Forever Hollywood*, a brilliant hour long documentary on the history of the movies. 6712 Hollywood Blvd. 323 466 3456

17 Les Deux Cafes (1997, Narduli/Grinstein) A piece of Provence in a tough Hollywood neighborhood: lush walled garden, remodeled craftsman house for indoor dining, brick walled cabaret. An in-place where name recognition is everything. 1638-40 N. Las Palmas Ave. 323 465 0509

18 Traction Designer/restaurateur Michele Lamy offers a personal selection of French eyeglasses, Lee Brevard's jewelery, and rare art books, plus traffic-stopping window displays. Open 3-8pm. 1643 N. Las Palmas Ave. 323 463 3700

19 Frances Goldwyn Regional Branch Library (1986, Frank O. Gehry & Associates) Shallow reflecting pools reflect light into this tight-walled cluster of stucco and glass boxes. 1623 Ivar St. 323 467 1821

20 Capitol Records (1956, Welton Becket) Cylindrical office tower suggests a stack of records topped by a stylus. Besides the promotional value, it offers, according to the architects, better energy conservation and more usable floor space than a conventional tower. 1750 Vine St.

21 Pantages Theater (1929, B. Marcus Priteca; decor by Anthony Heinsbergen) Movie palace turned Broadway musical showcase. It rivals the Wiltern as an anthology of zig zag moderne, from the vaulted lobby guarded by statues of a movie director and an aviatrix, to the amazing fretted ceiling of the auditorium. 6233 Hollywood Blvd. 323 468 1770

22 Angelil-Graham House (1993, Marc Angelil/Sarah Graham) T beam structure braced with tension cables at front and back, supporting a metal roof that floats over a two story box of rough wood. The steel columns are supported on concrete beams, 10 feet apart on center, which span three concrete retaining walls. 6009 Rodgerton Dr. at N. Beachwood Dr.

23 Samuels-Navarro House (1928, Lloyd Wright) Dramatically massed concrete and stucco house trimmed with pressed copper; upper and lower entrances. The long axis runs along a ridge from the garden through the house to the pool; a short cross axis terminates in the tower. 5609 Valley Oak Dr.

17 American Cinematheque

24 House (1996, William Adams) Canopied, wood-framed windows pop out of a cluster of gray stucco cubes flooding the interiors with light. 2165 Ponet Dr.

25 Sowden House (1926, Lloyd Wright) Courtyard house entered from a cavelike opening framed with decorative concrete blocks. 5121 Franklin Ave.

26 Ennis-Brown House (1924, Frank Lloyd Wright) From below, you see a cliff face of textile concrete blocks (cast on site and knitted together with reinforcing rods), but the interior is surprisingly cramped, with a few modest rooms opening off a linear corridor. Though urgently in need of restoration, it is the only FLW house in LA that is currently open for tours; M-Sa by reservation. 2655 Glendower Ave. 323 660 0607

Griffith Park Expansive hillside recreation area featuring sports of every kind, stables and hiking trails, the **LA Zoo**, the outdoor **Greek Theater**, and the **Gene Autry Western Heritage Museum**. Contact **Sunset Ranch** for their moonlit night rides to the top of the mountains. 323 469 5450

29 McAlmon House (1936, R. M. Schindler) Crisp white De Stijl composition with floating planes on a hillside above the street level garage/apartment. 2721 Waverly Dr.

30 Los Feliz Library (1999, Barton Phelps & Associates) A bold presence on the corner of two busy streets, a garden court in back to satisfy the competing urban/suburban demands of the community. Brilliant use of space, natural light and rich color within. 1874 Hillhurst Ave. at Franklin Ave. 323 913 4710

31 Vida Fred Eric's eclectic menu is served in a room lined with bamboo, another that's lacquered purple, or on a sunken table walled off by backlit screens. 1930 Hillhurst Ave. 323 660 4446

32 Franklin Ave Bridge (1926, J. C. Wright for City Engineer's Office) Gothic aedicules guard the ends of this graceful span. Between St. George St. & Myra Ave.

Silver Lake The houses scattered on the hills around this city reservoir and the winding streets

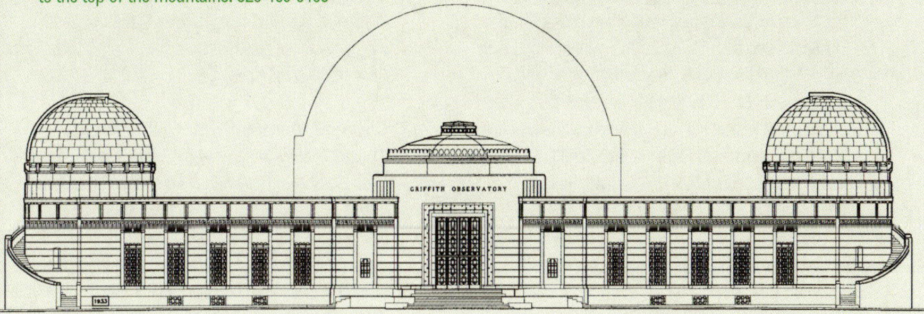

27 Griffith Observatory

27 Griffith Observatory & Planetarium (1935, John C. Austin & F. M. Ashley; to be restored and expanded 2002, Hardy Holzman Pfeiffer Associates) Copper domed, PWA moderne landmark; on a clear day, its terraces command a view of the entire city; at night you can often use the telescope. North end of Vermont Ave. 323 664 1191

28 Lovell Health House (1929, Richard Neutra) Steel framed, stucco-clad house with ribbon windows that launched Neutra's career. It remains one of the great icons of the International Style. You enter at the upper, bedroom level, descend into a cavernous living room, and down again to terraces and garden. Best seen from Aberdeen Ave, below. 4616 Dundee Dr.

that link them make this tight-knit community one of the most desirable in LA. In the '20s & '30s, it was a magnet for Schindler, Neutra, Ain, Harris, and other moderns, though most of their houses are well concealed. The greatest concentration is in the 2000-2400 blocks of Micheltorena St. Many hip boutiques have recently opened on Silver Lake Blvd, Hyperion & Rowena Aves.

33 CDLT 1, 2 House (1987-92, Michael Rotondi) The embodiment of chaos theory: a house that evolved piece by piece, without working drawings, as an ongoing experiment in living for the architect and his former wife. 1955 Cedar Lodge Terr.

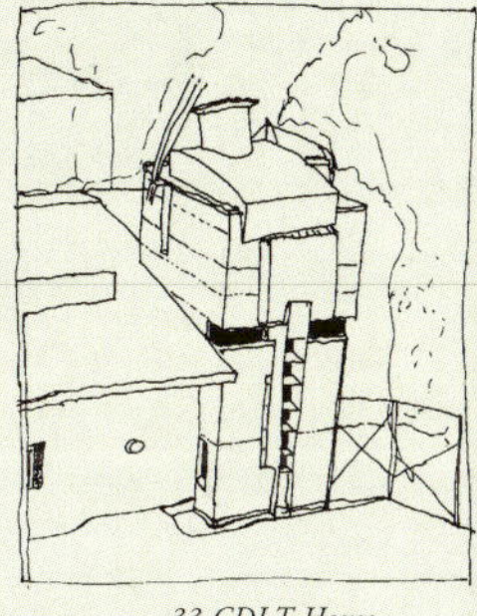

33 CDLT House

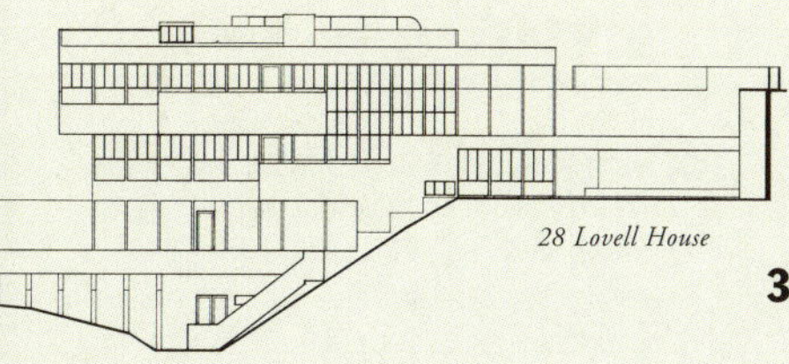

28 Lovell House

34 Andrew Dibben Trend setting men's clothing in an interior that presents changing art installations. W-Su, noon-6pm. 1618 Silver Lake Blvd. 323 662 9189

Black: exterior only, or open to public   **Blue:** interior; by appt. only   **Red:** private residence, do not disturb   **Green:** park, or public open space

35 Neutra VDL House (1966, Richard & Dion Neutra) Neutra created an experimental, machine-like house/studio for himself in 1933, and added a guest wing in 1939. It was destroyed by fire in 1963 and was rebuilt with his son, Dion. Currently run-down, it is being restored by the College of Environmental Design, California State Polytechnic University at Pomona. 2300 Silver Lake Blvd. Call 909 869 2667 to arrange a visit. Nine other post-war Neutra houses occupy the 2200 block of Silver Lake Blvd.

36 Hollyhock House (1917-20, Frank Lloyd Wright; restoration 2000-03; studio/residence A, garden wall & landscaping, R. M. Schindler) Oil heiress Aline Barnsdall commissioned this extraordinary house (named for an abstraction of the flower) as the center-piece of a planned arts center, little of which was built, and then bequeathed it to the city, which has proved an irresponsible custodian. Dedicated volunteers have long been frustrated by bureaucratic infighting and penny pinching; the 1994 earthquake exacerbated long standing problems and rain streamed through the roof for five years while committees dickered. As a result, the house requires major restoration and is likely to be closed at least through 2002. One can hope that the city will then turn it over to a non-profit private organization. (Another Wright house has been closed until further notice. For lack of funds, USC has allowed Wright's **Freeman House** to deteriorate alarmingly and is now planning to shore it up and find an appropriate custodian.) **Barnsdall Park** is being relandscaped by Walker & Associates, and may be closed through mid 2001. 4800 Hollywood Blvd.

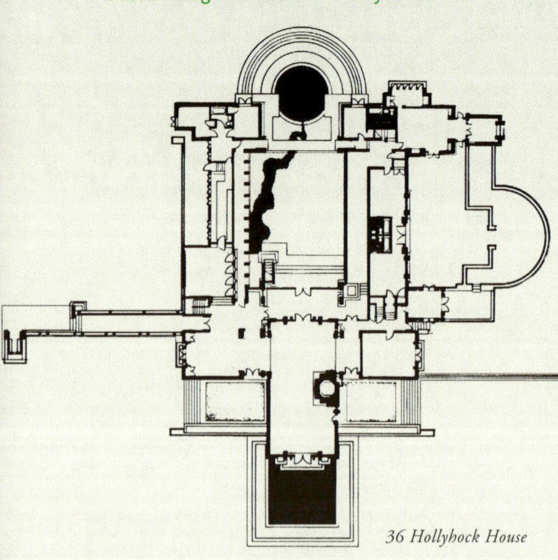

36 Hollyhock House

37 Klasky Csupo (2000, Area) A former Mercedes showroom remodeled for use by a film animation company. A galvanized steel wall separates the public area from the workspaces in the ovoid entrance. Behind is a whimsical indoor townscape of abstract forms and open workstations. 6353 Sunset Blvd. 323 463 0145

38 Crossroads of the World (1936, Robert Derrah) Fantasy shopping/office compound, evoking a streamline cruise ship in a port surrounded by English, French, Spanish and Moorish shops. 6671 Sunset Blvd. 323 463 5611

39 Villa d'Este (1928, Pierpont & Walter S. Davis) Best of several lushly planted courtyard apartments in this area which made inventive use of Mediterranean models through the '20s. 1355 Laurel Ave. Handsome neighbors include the **Ronda** and **Andalusia** on Havenhurst Dr, a block west.

40 Storer House (1923, Frank Lloyd Wright) Impeccably restored textile block house, more spacious and less idiosyncratic in its plan than the Ennis house. 8161 Hollywood Blvd.

Sunset Strip Concentration of rock clubs, restaurants, sidewalk cafes, chic shops, and vanity billboards catering to the heavy east-west, music-movie traffic between Hollywood and the Westside. It has recovered much of the prestige and glamour it lost in the '60s, and Sunset Plaza is fashion central with a cluster of crowded sidewalk eateries. Crescent Heights Blvd. to Doheny Dr.

41 Chateau Marmont Hotel (1929, Arnold Weitzman; 1956 bungalows by Craig Ellwood; restored 1995-97, Shawn Hausman & Fernando Santangelo) Unlike Norma Desmond, this local version of a Loire chateau is a star that has aged gracefully, attracting every famous name in the business, from Garbo on. It was threadbare when Andre Balazs bought it, but he wisely decided to keep its funky character, while subtly refurbishing it. The **Bar Marmont**, next door, has an exotic decor based on a scene cut from Coppola's *Apocalypse Now*. 8221 Sunset Lane. 323 656 1010

42 The Standard (1999, Shawn Hausman) Low cost, high style alternative to the Marmont: a second Balazs makeover that retains the wavy '60s balconies of the former Thunderbird Motel and creates a sexy white stage set (plus blue astroturf around the pool) for the young and hip to strut. 8300 Sunset Blvd. 323 650 9090

43 Argyle Hotel (1931, Leland A. Bryant; restored and remodeled 1989, David Lawrence Gray; interiors by David Becker) Built as a prestigious 12 story apartment tower with rounded and angled bays, and a froth of art deco ornament, it was revived as a boutique hotel. Retro decor and spectacular views. The poolside bar overlooking the lights of LA is the place to be. 8358 Sunset Blvd. 323 654 7100

44 Mondrian Hotel (1996, Philippe Starck) Chic French version of heaven, with staff in designer whites, and hip guests in black, drifting languidly through a succession of provocatively furnished indoor and outdoor rooms. Long table for casual dining in lobby; **Asia de Cuba** (323 848 6000) serves fusion fare in a room that seems to float above the city and on a terrace flanked by huge flower pots. The

Black: exterior only, or open to public **Blue:** interior; by appt. only **Red:** private residence, do not disturb **Green:** park, or public open space

Sky Bar is a hot night spot, lofted above the pool court. As with heaven, only the chosen few may enter. 8440 Sunset Blvd. 323 650 8999

45 Sunset Marquis (Refurbished 1999, Oliva Villaluz, Barry Salehian) A production designer collaborated with an architect to refine the luxurious interior of this discreet all-suites hotel which draws the top names of the industry. 1200 N. Alta Loma Rd. 310 657 1333

46 Oliver Peoples (1996, Ilan Dei) Cool room, stylish eyeglasses, excellent service. 8642 Sunset Blvd. 310 657 2553

47 Delvaux (1996, CSC) Light-filled, satinwood showcase for fine Belgian leather goods; dramatic staircase. 8647 Sunset Blvd. 310 289 8588

47 Domont Highly regarded source for vintage Chanel costume jewelry, contemporary couture jewelry from France and Italy, and the designs of Iradg. 8661 Sunset Blvd. 310 289 9500

48 Book Soup Outstanding selection of books and magazines; distinctive restaurant; parking in back. 8818 Sunset Blvd. 310 659 3110

49 Fire Station #7 (1999, Gonzalez/Goodale Architects) Handsome wood-frame corner building with a high level of transparency, a clerestory-lit dormitory tucked beneath a high arched vault over the engine shed, and offices to the rear, where the vault descends to respect the residential scale of a side street. 864 W. San Vicente Blvd.

50 Click Model Management (1991, Hodgetts + Fung) Complex, light-filled spaces set atop a ground floor garage. Three complementary volumes (lobby, offices, conference room, services) are enclosed within a narrow rectilinear box of concrete block and glass and linked by a bridge/terrace. 9057 Nemo St. 310 246 0800

51 Margo Leavin Gallery (1984-89, David Serrurier) Inspired conversion of two wood-vaulted lofts, built by Norma Talmadge and Merle Oberon respectively, for changing exhibitions of work by top contemporary artists. One of these, Claes Oldenburg, has created a trompe l'oeil facade for the Hilldale building: a knife slicing through the wall. 812 N. Robertson Blvd. & 817 N. Hilldale Ave. 310 273 0603

52 Ramada West Hollywood (1990, Oved/ Zimmerman with Francesca Garcia-Marques) Twin barrel vaulted volumes push forward to the sidewalk and frame a landscaped entrance courtyard with a colorful sculpture by Peter Shire. Stylish lobby; small but serviceable rooms. 8585 Santa Monica Blvd. 310 652 6400

53 L'Orangerie Unabashedly grand and retro. The classic French cuisine is consistently great, and the service is impeccable. A guilty and costly pleasure for modernists. 903 N. La Cienega Blvd. 310 652 9770

53 Wolper on Two Peruvian figurines, Panamanian baskets, and French Art Deco cabinets are featured in this new showroom which plans to stay open late every day of the week. 855 N. La Cienega Blvd. 310 659 7772

54 Algabar An exceptional selection of French and Asian furniture, pillows, decorative accessories, and linens. 920 N. La Cienega Blvd. 310 360 3500

55 West Hollywood City Hall (1995, Mehrdad Yazdani/Ellerbe Becket) Sharp new metal, glass, and integrally colored stucco skin applied to a mediocre commercial block, which has been remodeled to consolidate the city's administration and create a civic amenity. 8300 Santa Monica Blvd.

56 Felt (2000, Ralph Gentile/Sophie Harvey) Felt-lined interior, in brown and orange with moody lighting, and a bamboo-shaded patio, create a setting for Bobby Cocca's light, healthy fare. 8279 Santa Monica Blvd.

57 Linn House AIDS Hospice (1996, Cavaedium) Exemplary urban design: a 25 bed institution that is cleverly massed to suggest three traditional houses in scale with their neighbors. The steel frame is quietly expressed as part of the cream and khaki stucco facade. Each resident has a private room, opening onto balcony or patio. 1001 Martel Ave. at Romaine St.

58 Propaganda Films (1988, Franklin D. Israel) An interior village of sculptural enclosures within the blank walled shell of a warehouse provides flexible office and meeting spaces for a progressive film production company. 940 N. Mansfield Ave. 323 462 6400

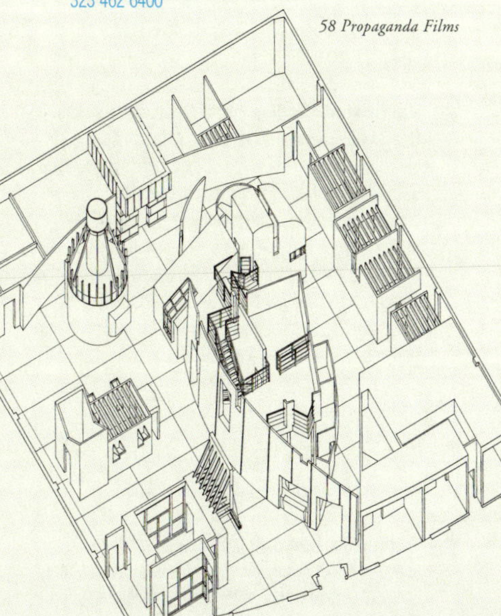

58 Propaganda Films

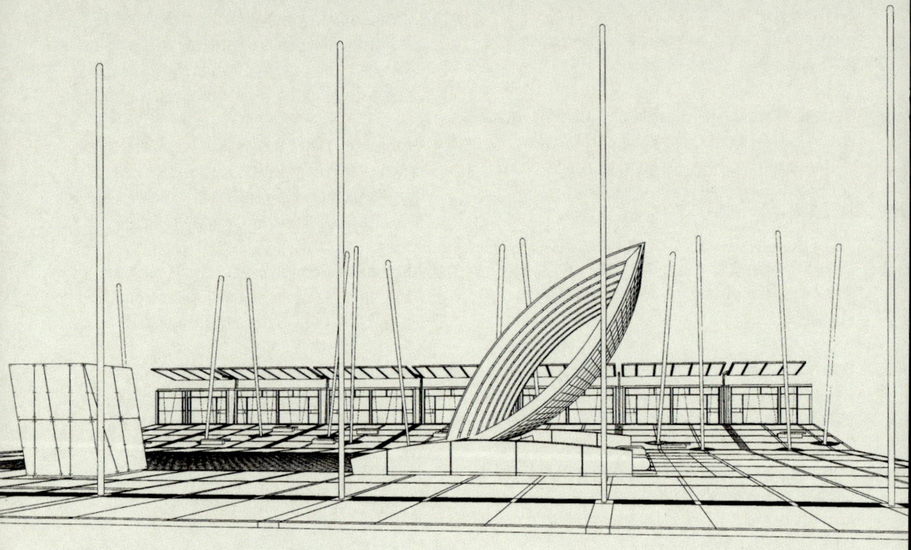

59 Vermont/Santa Monica Station

59 Vermont/Santa Monica Station (1994-99, Mehrdad Yazdani/Ellerbe Becket with Robert Millar) The one outstanding Metro station. An elliptical metal canopy hovers over the entry down to a grand concrete hall lit from glass blocks set into a plaza/performance space with lights set on canted poles. Millar integrated his powerful artwork with the structure. Vermont Ave. & Santa Monica Blvd.

Melrose Ave. The hippest street in LA in the '80s; it has since choked on its own success. Too many gawkers and too little parking, especially on weekends. Most trend-setters have moved on to La Brea and Beverly Blvd, but there's still plenty to do and see.

60 Newspace Minimal and eclectic art by Martha Alf, Alan Wayne, Kristin Leachman and others. Open Tu-Sa, 11am-4pm. 5241 Melrose Ave, 3 blocks E. of Vine. 323 469 9353

61 Paramount Studios Last of the major studios in Hollywood. The original entrance gate can still be glimpsed from Melrose; the stage topped with a globe at the corner of Gower once belonged to RKO. The blank facade of an archive building just inside the main entrance is painted as a sky in case the real thing isn't good enough. 5555 Melrose Ave. Across the street is the **Raleigh Rental Studio**; behind its new stages is a street lined with wood framed cottages that seems unchanged from 1915.

62 Morgan House (1917, Irving Gill) Two round arches frame the side drive; windows sit high on the chaste white concrete walls; there's little to see, but what is there is choice. 626 N. Arden Blvd.

63 Patina (Remodeled 2000, Belzberg Architects) Joaquim Splichal's inspired cuisine has a new setting: a modular steel facade with cedar slats that open up the refined interior with its hardwood paneling, limestone pavers, and elegant furniture. 5955 Melrose Ave. 323 467 1108

64 Citrus (1987, Bernard Zimmerman) An airy, all-white shed with glass brick walls, enlivened by fresh flowers and colorful paintings, and a patio shaded by white umbrellas, provide the setting for delectable California cuisine. 6703 Melrose Ave. 323 657 0034

65 Danziger Studio (1965, Frank O. Gehry & Associates) Three blank stucco boxes, adroitly positioned to conceal entrance and windows, transform LA's industrial vernacular into high art. 7001 Melrose Ave.

66 Circa 1910 A great place to furnish an Arts and Crafts home—with oak furniture, hammered copper, pottery, and paintings. 7206 Melrose Ave. 323 965 1910

66 Denny Burt Depression ware, art glass, and modern antiques. 7208 Melrose Ave. 323 936 5269

67 Laca (2000, Ralph Gentile and Sophie Harvey) Sophisticated French cooking by Warren Schwartz, formerly of Patina, in an elegant setting of antique terracotta, oak cabinetry, raw silk curtains and candlelight, with a charming patio. 7250 Melrose Ave.

67 Angeli Caffe (1982, Morphosis) Earthy Italian food in an early deconstructivist interior; excessively noisy. 7274 Melrose Ave. 323 936 9086

68 l.a. Eyeworks Gai Gerhardi and Barbara McReynolds pioneered Melrose in 1979 and have been designing cutting-edge eyewear ever since. They have commissioned Zaha Hadid to design a new store, her first, at 7386 Beverly Blvd. Let's hope it happens. 7407 Melrose Ave. 323 653 8255

Black: exterior only, or open to public **Blue:** interior; by appt. only **Red:** private residence, do not disturb **Green:** park, or public open space

69 Optical Shop of Aspen High end designer brands including Matsuda, Clayton Franklin, Hiero, and BKC. 7580 Melrose Ave. 323 653 5238

70 Emmerson Troop William Emmerson's functional and whimsical furniture is mixed in with vintage steel furniture, and pieces by Thonet, Paul Frankel, and Paul McCobb. 7957 Melrose Ave. 323 653 9763

70 Liza Bruce (1999, Alvis Vega) Exquisite swimwear and lingerie set off by a palette-sheet interior that uses mirrors to create an illusion of space. 7977 Melrose Ave. 323 655 5012

71 Costume National (2000, Marmol & Radziner) Sophisticated, cutting-edge Italian fashion for men and women in a striking architectural space divided up with glass, stainless steel, and lacquered panels. 8001 Melrose Ave. 323 655 8160

71 Plug Pia Deleon and Lori Bush make a personal choice of lighting by Italian, English and French designers; plus a surreal 1937 creation by Salvador Dali for Jean-Michel Frank. 8017 Melrose Ave. 323 653 5635

71 Miu Miu Hip Italian fashion for young women— a clone of Prada in a huge white skylit loft. 8025 Melrose Ave. 323 651 0072

72 Pegaso International Eugenio Manzoni and Brian Pinto sell mid-century Italian furnishings by Gio Ponti, Caslo Mollino, and Ettore Sottsass. 8117 Melrose Ave. 323 655 8117

72 Russell Simpson Furniture by William Haines, Edward Wormsley, and Pierre Paulin is regularly featured in this recently enlarged showroom which specializes in the '50s and '60s. 8121 Melrose Ave. 323 651 3992

72 Darryl K (1999, The Drezner Group) Edgy, contemporary sportswear in a subtly inflected white box. 8125 Melrose Ave. 323 651 2251

73 Fred Segal Youth-oriented emporium, with separate rooms for every kind of clothing. 8100 Melrose Ave. 323 651 4129. Eat all'Italiana in **Mauro's Cafe**. 323 653 9970

74 Jenny Armit Top London designer shows her own furnishings, and one-off or limited edition pieces by Jasper Morrison, Mathew Hilton, Tom Dixon, Danny Lane and other trendy Brits. 8210 Melrose Ave. 323 782 9173

74 Decades (1999, Iris Fingerhut) Upstage your fashionista friends in a '60s vintage Ossie Clark, Paco Rabanne or Andre Courreges dress, which you can find in the chic upstairs salon. At street level, **Decades Two** (323 655 1960) offers bargain resales on nearly new clothing and accessories from Prada, Chanel, and Gucci. 8214 Melrose Ave. 323 655 0223

75 Aesthetic Frame & Art Services Fine tailoring for your favorite works of art. 8221 Melrose Ave. 323 653 9033

76 Pieces Dianne Carr shows a wide range of conservative, contemporary furniture which can be customized on request. 8280 Melrose Ave. 323 653 0808

77 Kiho Higashi Minimal and reductive art, including work by Larry Bell, Max Cole and Carolee Toon. 8332 Melrose Ave. 323 655 2482

77 Jozu (Remodeled 2000, Merry Norris with Johnson, Favaro) Andy Nakano is the amiable host at this serene retreat serving refined Franco-Asian dishes. 8360 Melrose Ave. 323 655 5600

78 MAK Center/Schindler House (1922, R. M. Schindler) Inspired by a camping trip in Yosemite, Schindler built this extraordinary house/commune for two couples, with tilt-up concrete slab walls around the perimeter, rooftop sleeping canopies, and an interplay of outdoor and indoor space. Sensitively restored, with a new office by COA. MAK (Austrian Museum of Applied Art) currently administers the house as a study/exhibition center. Open to the public W-Su, 11am-6pm. 835 N. Kings Rd. 323 651 1510

79 Thanks for the Memories The finest streamline furniture and collectibles at prices to match. 8319 Melrose Ave. 323 852 9407

80 Gemini GEL (1976, Frank O. Gehry & Associates) For 30 years, such leading artists as Richard Serra, Robert Rauschenberg, Ellsworth Kelly, and David Hockney have come here to make their finest prints. M-Fr 9:30-5pm. 8365 Melrose Ave. 323 651 0513

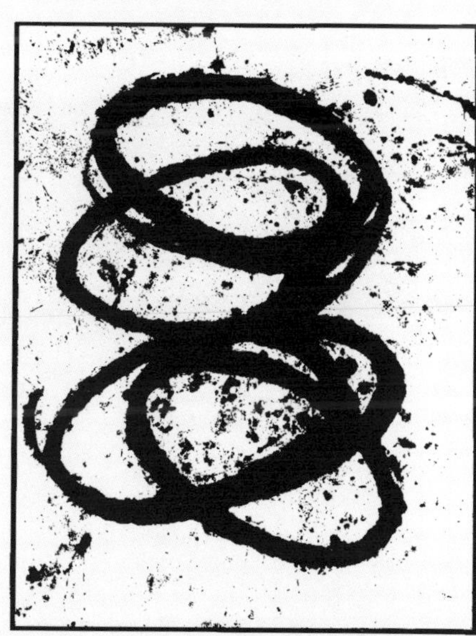

80 T. E. Sparrows © Richard Serra/Gemini GEL

81 City Studio Elegant, Deco-inspired furniture. 8444 Melrose Ave. 323 658 6354

81 Lucques (1998, Barbara Barry) Rave notices (and big crowds) for the gutsy southern French food; eat in the intimate, brick walled dining room or elegant canopied courtyard. 8474 Melrose Ave. 323 655 6277

81 Ago (1997, Ralph Gentile Sophie Harvey) Open truss steel roof and buttery stucco walls provide a handsome backdrop for this celebrity sponsored, Tuscan restaurant. 8478 Melrose Ave. 323 655 6333

82 James Jennings Custom furniture by Jennings, Kerry Joyce, and Madeline Stewart, all with a neo-classical flavor. 8471 Melrose Ave. 323 655 7823

82 Ann Sacks Ceramic, limestone and porcelain tiles from Italy, France and Spain, plus custom designs from domestic manufacturers. 8483 Melrose Ave, NE corner La Cienega Blvd. 323 658 8884

83 Barokh On a street selling high end antiques, this is one of the best, specializing in 17th and 18th century Italian furniture. 8481 Melrose Pl. 323 655 2771

84 Downtown Vintage modern and contemporary crafts with an Asian touch. 719 N. La Cienega Blvd. 310 652 7461

84 Alto Palato Mixed reviews for this restaurant which offers Wednesday dinners from different regions of Italy in a handsome, lofty space with patio seating. 755 N. La Cienega Blvd. 310 657 9271

85 Blackman Cruz Huge clocks, exotic metal furniture, and many other one of a kind pieces to give interiors a lift. 800 N. La Cienega Blvd. 310 657 9228

86 Center for Early Education (1988, Goldman/Firth/Boccato) Three story stucco classroom blocks with rooftop playgrounds, linked by a steel-framed glass atrium. Playful use of color and gables; serpentine brick wall wrapped around sidewalk palms. 563 N. Alfred St.

87 Art Wares Laura Newman makes a discerning selection of baskets, ceramics, glass, and wood objects. 8625 Melrose Ave. 310 652 6428

87 Details Cutting-edge door furniture and other architectural accessories. 8625 ½ Melrose Ave. 310 659 1550

88 Soolip Paperie & Press Handmade papers, elegant cards, and a small gallery for works on paper in back. 8646 Melrose Ave. 310 360 0545. Close by is **Soolip-Marie Papier**; intensely colored papers and notebooks from Paris. 8574 Melrose Ave. 310 360 0581

88 Robert Kuo An update on traditional Chinese furniture, tableware and jewelery, plus Tang pottery and other Pan-Asian antiques. 8686 Melrose Ave. 310 855 1555

89 Pacific Design Center (1975-88, Cesar Pelli/Gruen Associates; refurbished 2000, Area) Huge shiny blue and green glass containers for the largest concentration of wholesale interior design showrooms in the West. Open to all for browsing M-F, 9am-5pm; purchases must be made through design professionals. For referrals, contact the concierge service. Charles Cohen, the new owner who turned around the D & D Building in New York, has announced major improvements to reinvigorate the Blue Whale, and plans to lease most of Center Green as offices. 8687 Melrose Ave. 310 657 0800

Standouts among PDC's 130 tenants include many of the top names in fine fabrics: **The Bradbury Collection** 310 657 3940; **Donghia** 310 657 6060; **Kneedler Fauchere** 310 855 1313; **Oakmont** 310 659 1423; **Randolph & Hein** 310 855 1222; **Scalamandre** 310 657 8154; **F. Schumacher** 310 652 5353. For furniture, **Dakota Jackson** (1998, Peter Eisenman) is the best looking showroom;

89 Don Chadwick sofa / Forms and Surfaces

Black: exterior only, or open to public **Blue:** interior; by appt. only **Red:** private residence, do not disturb **Green:** park, or public open space

see also, for top modern designers, **Forms and Surfaces** 310 659 9134; and **Janus et Cie** 310 652 7090 for elegant patio furniture. For contract furniture, **Vitra** 310 652 7997 and **ICF Group** 310 659 0733 have a modest presence. More traditional furniture is on show at **Baker Knapp & Tubbs** 310 652 7252 and **Mimi London** 310 855 2567. For upscale kitchens, one can choose from **Cooper Pacific** 310 659 6147; **Poggenpohl** 310 289 4901; and **Snaidero** 310 657 5497. Also of note are **International Down & Linen** 310 657 8243; **Charles Jacobsen** antiques 310 652 1188; **Stark Carpets** 310 657 8275; **Knoll** 310 289 5800, the last major contract firm in the PDC, is relocating to Santa Monica.

Several design organizations are located in the PDC. **LA Chapter/AIA** (1995, Coe Design) deftly combines offices, meeting and exhibit areas, making inventive use of metal and translucent glass. 310 785 1809. On the plaza that extends to San Vicente Blvd. is the **Murray Feldman Gallery**, which will become an architecture and design satellite gallery for MOCA; check PDC for schedule.

89 **Dailey & Associates** (1997, Christine Chatterton & Associates) For a top ad agency, the designer cannibalized eight former showrooms along the 3rd floor concourse of the PDC's Center Green, creating an indoor village with a wonderful mish mash of found decor, pulled together by taut vinyl membranes that float below the exposed ductwork. Dailey CEO Cliff Einstein has added contemporary artwork from his outstanding collection. 310 360 3655

90 **Workhouse** (1996, Guthrie & Buresh) Two innovative architects have created an intricate studio/house for themselves from raw plywood and plexi. 528 N. San Vicente Blvd.

90 Workhouse

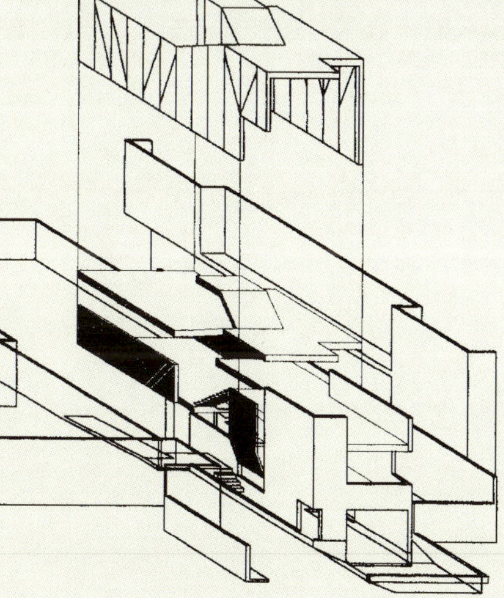

91 **Waterworks** Tiles and plumbing fixtures for sybaritic bathrooms. 8715 Melrose Ave. 310 289 5211

91 **J. Robert Scott** Sally Sirkin Lewis designed the cool modern showroom, which presents a vast array of traditional fabrics and furnishings. 8737 Melrose Ave. 310 659 4910

92 **Walker & Zanger** A great source for granite, marble, limestone, and slate. 8750 Melrose Ave. 310 659 1234

93 **Anichini** Exclusive Italian bed and table linens including rare antiques. 466 N. Robertson Blvd. 310 657 4292

93 **Remba** A facade by Jonathan Borowsky of animated bronze turtles draws attention to this gallery, which specializes in prints by contemporary Latin American and Korean artists. 462 N. Robertson Blvd. 310 657 1101

93 **Koplin** James Doolin, Kerry James Marshall, and David Ligare are among the contemporary realist painters and sculptors shown here. 464 N. Robertson Blvd. 310 657 9843

93 **Anne Hauk** French Art Deco furniture, decorative arts and jewelry of the '20s and '30s, plus paintings from Russia and Denmark. 458 N. Robertson Blvd. 310 659 3606

94 **Maxfield** (1986, Larry Totah) Ruinously expensive couture for men and women (Gaultier, Helmut Lang, Jil Sander, etc.) in a spare concrete shell, plus pricey vintage Hermes objects and other covetables. 8825 Melrose Ave. 310 274 8800

95 **Yujean Kang** Minimalist decor and superb contemporary Chinese cooking with specialties from different regions. 8826 Melrose Ave. 310 288 0806

96 **Decorative Carpets** Vast selection, on the walls and in catalogues, including the Tufekian Tibetan rugs designed by Barbara Barry and others. 8900 Melrose Ave. 310 859 6330

96 **Chacmool** Kenneth Noland, Mary Corse, and Dernar Venet are among the artists regularly shown at a gallery specializing in abstract painting and sculpture. 8920 Melrose Ave. 310 550 6792

97 **Regen Projects** Eclectic mix of media, featuring younger and mid-career artists. 629 N. Almont Dr. 310 276 5424

97 **Manny Silverman** American abstract art of the New York school. 619 N. Almont Dr. 310 659 8256

he Valley (as in "Valley Girl") is the name that distinguishes this sprawling expanse of single-family homes and commercial strips from other valleys in the region. Early settlements and farmland were gobbled up in the post war explosion of suburbia, leaving little of historic interest. Once overwhelmingly white and middle class, the Valley has now lost its homogeneity, but activists are pushing for secession from LA, arguing for the incorporation of a new city of two million. Architecturally, the pickings are slim, but there is a wonderful concentration of Schindler houses in Studio City, and the older strips rival those of Burbank as treasuries of Googie style.

1 **Universal Studios** Rios Associates have made some significant contributions to the public sector of this 90 year old movie studio, including the **Terminator 2: 3D** attraction with its skin of colored pixels and "morphing liquid metal"; the **Toll Plaza** with its dark blue steel canopy; and the **Pedestrian Bridge** enclosed with sheets of perforated aluminum. Nancy Goslee Power created a "cinematic landscape" in the arrivals area. Rem Koolhas was commissioned to develop a master plan pulling together the fragmented production/office facilities, amphitheater and entertainment/retail facilities.

1 **Universal City Walk** (1993-2000, Jerde Partnership) A zoo for that endangered species, the carefree pedestrian. No panhandling, litter, or crime in this tightly run replica of a real street, which has recently been expanded with new graphics by Sussman/Prejza. City Walk is a simplified version of Jerde's **Horton Plaza** in San Diego: a spatially varied pedestrian promenade, linking Universal Studios' theme park to the 18 screen Cineplex and Amphitheater. Within the structural frame, tenants have built-out their storefronts, notably Barbara Lazaroff's exuberant facade and tiled interior for the **Wolfgang Puck Cafe** (818 985 9653), and Sam Lopata's nautically themed **Gladstone's** (818 622 3474). The classic neon signs were restored by the Museum of Neon Art. Rios Associates redesigned Mehrdad Yazdani's **Showscan Emaginator Theater** ride simulator, adding dense layered graphics to its folded planes. 1000 Universal Center Dr, off the Ventura Fwy. 818 622 4455

1 **Universal Metro Station** (2000, Siegel Diamond Architecture with Margaret Garcia) A people-mover will link the station to Universal Studios, encouraging visitors to take the Metro and avoid the hassle of parking. Architect and artist collaborated to celebrate the history of the site—which is where the last

Mexican governor of California signed the treaty ceding authority to the Yankees. Lankershim Blvd. at Universal Pl.

2 **Ivan Reitman Productions** (1994, Barton Myers Associates) Executive offices, editing and screening rooms for one of Hollywood's most successful producer/directors: pure modern in the land of make believe. Across from the New York Street and a Federal-style church on the Universal back lot stand crisp cement plaster and glass cubes, which define a north-facing courtyard with a view to the mountains. Can be seen from the parking lot to the north of the back lot.

3 **Hanna Barbera** (1995, Coe Design) For the makers of *The Jetsons*, a colorful piece of pop futurism in cartoon colors remodeled from existing buildings. 3400 Cahuenga Blvd.

4 **Fredonia Apartments** (1964, Raymond Kappe) 12 unit building that brilliantly exploits a hillside site. Six duplex studios echo the curve of the drive; single story units are built over the garage. All units have patios. 3625 Fredonia Dr.

4 **Kallis House** (1946-51, R. M. Schindler) It's easy to see where the current obsession with folded planes began—in this tiny, sensitively restored jewel. 3580 Multiview Dr.

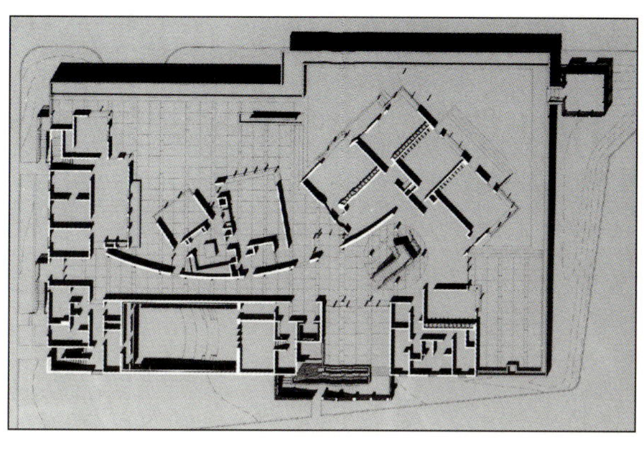

2 Ivan Reitman Productions

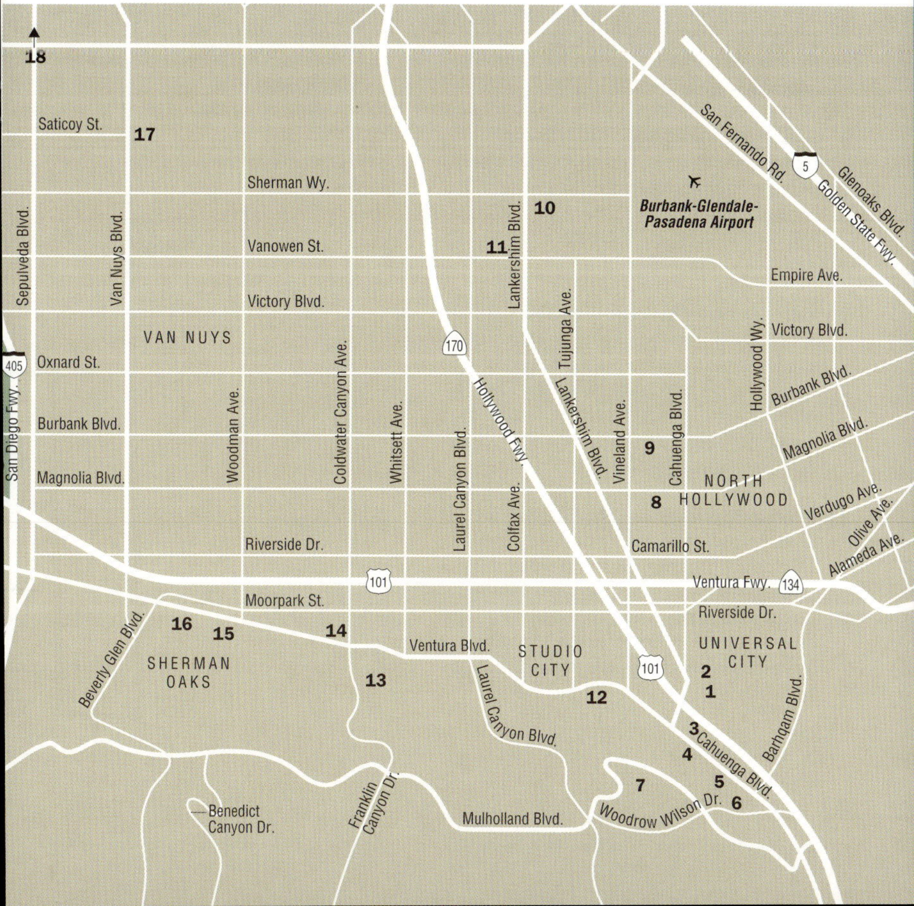

5 World Supply Architects and designers, as well as artists, find what they need in this well-stocked emporium. 3425 W. Cahuenga Blvd at Universal Center Dr. 323 851 1350

6 Viso House (1990, Hodgetts + Fung) Colored stucco cubes, clinging to a steep hillside, enclose interlocking volumes that open off a cylindrical hub; Schindler's influence is evident. 2911 Viso Dr.

Mulholland Drive Scenic highway that winds 50 miles from just north of the Hollywood Bowl to the Pacific along the crest of the Santa Monica mountains. You can park in overlooks and enjoy sweeping views across LA and the Valley, especially on clear winter days or when the Santa Ana winds blow.

7 Chemosphere House (1960, John Lautner; restored 1999, Escher GuneWardena) Commissioned by an aerospace engineer, this architect's most dramatic structure has been imaginatively restored for a German publisher with a passion for modern design. A self-operated funicular carries one to the top of a concrete mushroom; canted windows set into the arched vault of laminated beams command sweeping views of hills and the Valley. The house can be glimpsed from the 7800 block of the street below. 7776 Torreyson Dr, off Mulholland Dr.

8 Arte de Mexico Huge emporium crammed with vintage doors, chandeliers, and other architectural elements from south of the border. 5356 Riverton Ave, North Hollywood. 818 769 5090

9 Scavengers Paradise Mid-century Spanish and modern architectural fragments, from plumbing fixtures to wrought iron gates and stained glass, fountains and columns. 5453 Satsuma Ave , 2 blocks E. of Vineland, $1/2$ block S. of Burbank, North Hollywood. 323 877 7945

10 Kaiser Regional Reference Laboratory (1995, Stone Marraccini Patterson) Sleek glass and gray steel curtain wall, punctuated by projecting stair towers; the muscular structural frame of yellow steel I beams is visible behind. The interior is orchestrated to create a sense of community. 11668 Sherman Way, North Hollywood. 818 503 6568

11 DWP North Hollywood Pump Station (1992, Barton Phelps & Associates) The massive concrete box containing the pumps that transfer water from the LA Aqueduct to the central city is treated as a billboard, with an incised map, tiled ocean, and boldly-scaled lettering. Desert landscaping reinforces the message of water as the key to survival. 11803 Vanowen St.

12 Sushi Nozawa Arguably the best sushi in LA, created as a work of art by a perfectionist. 11288 Ventura Blvd, Studio City. 818 508 7017

13 Harvard-Westlake Art Center (1998, Michael Maltzan) The Feldman-Horn Center for the Arts resembles Inner City Arts in the way it creates a sense of place and ties together scattered buildings by expressing the new gallery, studios, and classrooms for this private school as a cluster of skewed, white stucco volumes. 3700 Coldwater Canyon, North Hollywood. 818 980 6692

14 Pinot Bistro (1992, Cheryl Brantner) Traditional Parisian bistro with reminders (including a Man Ray room) of the artists who once frequented them. The menu also puts a spin on tradition. 12969 Ventura Blvd, Studio City. 818 990 0500

15 Weiss House (1991, Michael Folonis) Copper-clad roof cascades down over steel-troweled plaster walls, in this inventive remodel/expansion of an existing house. 4070 Benedict Canyon, Sherman Oaks.

16 Café Bizou Wildly popular French bistro, with bargain prices and a $2 corkage charge. 14016 Ventura Blvd, E. of Hazeltine, Sherman Oaks. 818 788 3536

17 Van Nuys Distribution HQ (1992, Ellerbe Becket/Mehrdad Yazdani) Another award-winning facility for the ubiquitous DWP, comprising offices, warehouse, and assembly room, which makes good use of concrete block, stucco, and painted metal panels. 14401 Saticoy St, Van Nuys.

Black: exterior only, or open to public **Blue:** interior; by appt. only **Red:** private residence, do not disturb **Green:** park, or public open space

18 Sepulveda Recreation Center (1995, Koning Eizenberg) Colored and pierced concrete block walls and bowed vault enclose a gym, community rooms, and other facilities; a low budget addition to a tough neighborhood park. 8825 Kester Ave, Sepulveda.

19 Sepulveda Dam Lean, elegant product of '30s engineers, which can be glimpsed from the transition from the San Diego to the Ventura freeways, heading west, or on foot from the Sepulveda Dam Recreation Area.

20 Ten db (1998, CSC Architecture) Raw-edged loft space for an editing company created by stripping a '60s office building to its structural frame and walling the north-facing street facade with glass. 15422 Ventura Blvd, Sherman Oaks. 818 728 7300

21 Aris Vision Center (1999, Michelle Anaya) Laser vision correction center featuring curved glazed walls, slate and bamboo floors, plus fountains, maple furnishings and a good selection of art to soften the impact of high technology. 16952 Ventura Blvd, Encino. 818 205 1565

22 The Dye Building (1991, Arkineto/Mark Fuote) Three story retail/office building, sharply angled to maximize the number of corner offices and to stand out

from its drab neighbors. Windows and balconies are set back behind an exposed structural frame. 19019 Ventura Blvd, Tarzana.

23 Struckus House (1982-92, Bruce Goff) Steel-reinforced plywood cylinder, clad in wood and stucco, with a stack of four front windows like lidded eyes. A central spiral stair links the four levels. Goff sketched this house just before his death; the owner, a rocket engineer, built it. 4510 Saltillo St, Woodland Hills.

24 Warner Park Pavilion (1993, Jeffrey Kalban & Assoc) Exemplary outdoor performance stage, with a tensile canopy and bowed walls that suggest a proscenium arch. 21820 W. Califa Ave, off Topanga Canyon Blvd, Woodland Hills.

25 Chatsworth MTA Train Depot & Child Care Center (1996, Alex Istanbullu & John Kaliski) Commuter station that evokes the old Southern Pacific Depot to the west, but shifts scale and vocabulary to create an intimate play area outside the classrooms to the east. 21510 Devonshire St, Chatsworth.

13 Harvard-Westlake Art Center

Beverly Hills is a model of urban planning that has filled out and matured over almost a century. The "Golden Triangle" of upscale shops divides the modest homes and apartments to the south of Wilshire from the mansions to the north, and the estates on the streets that wind up into the hills above Sunset Blvd. There was even an industrial zone served by a rail line that ran along the median strip of Santa Monica Blvd—once the final lap of Route 66. Huge trees, luxuriant gardens, and wide roads frame surprisingly rustic houses, mostly Spanish in style, with the odd vulgarity to disturb the tranquility. The prewar commercial buildings have a naïve charm, but glitz and PoMo historicism is taking over on the smarter shopping streets. The ersatz creaky tramcar carrying its riders back to the happy days of yore is laughable.

5 Pratesi The finest, best detailed and costliest, Italian table and bed linens. 9024 Burton Way, at Weatherby. 310 274 7661

6 L'Ermitage Beverly Hills (1998, Chhada Simbieda Remedios) Serene, spacious business hotel with an Asian flair; wood, stone, and silk contribute to the understated elegance. 9291 Burton Way at Maple-Rexford. 310 278 3344

7 Litton Industries (1937, Paul Williams) Federal Revival office building with a grand portico and lantern —a major work by this prolific, eclectic African-American architect. 360 N. Crescent Dr.

8 Union 76 Gas Station (1965, Gin Wong/Pereira & Luckman) Swooping cantilevered concrete canopy with integrated fluorescent lighting; a period classic. Rexford Dr. at S. Santa Monica Blvd.

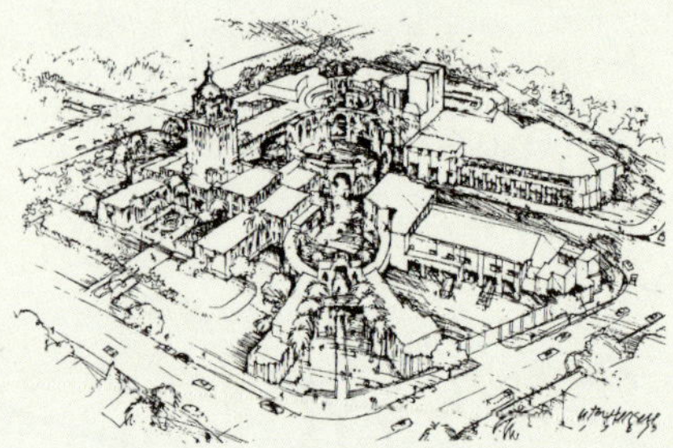

1 Beverly Hills Civic Center

1 Beverly Hills Civic Center (1988-92, Charles Moore/UIG) Brilliant concept subverted by municipal incompetence and parsimony. Moore won a competition with his design for a diagonal sequence of three landscaped courtyards that would link a new library, fire and police stations, offices, and parking to the restored **City Hall** (1932, William J. Gage). Key elements, including a theater and water course, were eliminated; finishes cheapened, and a road was driven like a stake through its heart. Repetitive deco detailing looks very thin beside the rich baroque scrolls of City Hall. Santa Monica Blvd at Rexford Dr.

2 The Ice House (1993, Barton Myers Associates) Imaginatively recycled industrial plant with an elegant new facade of steel and sandblasted glass. 9348 Civic Center Dr.

3 Virgin Records (1991 Franklin D. Israel Design Associates) A billowing curve of terracotta stucco, cut away to reveal a desert garden, heralds this adventurous remodel of a cavernous warehouse. Within, a short axis leads to a cylindrical amphitheater and a long cross axis lined with offices. 338 N. Foothill Rd. 310 278 1181

4 Maple Drive (1989, Anthony Greenberg) Understated elegance for a fashionable crowd. Oysters and meatloaf are standouts; jazz nightly. 345 N. Maple Dr. 310 274 9800

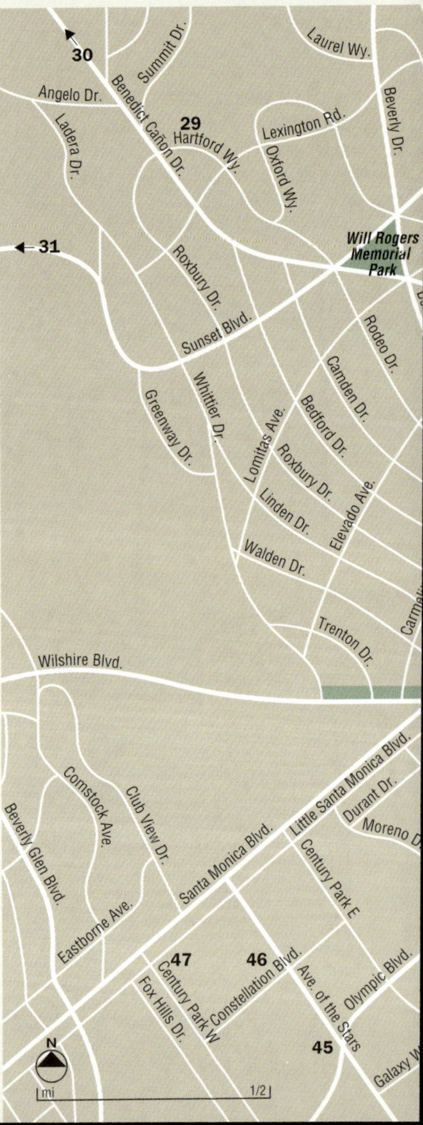

9 Spago Beverly Hills (1997, Barbara Lazaroff/ Imaginings Interior Design with Stephen F. Jones) Flamboyant, art filled public and private dining rooms, plus bar, opening up to three sides of a brick paved, tree shaded terrace. A celebrity-studded crowd enjoys Wolfgang Puck's superb French/California cuisine; reserve far ahead. 176 N. Canon Dr. 310 385 0880

10 Grant Selwyn Gallery (1999, Frederick Fisher & Partners) Minimalist setting for minimal and conceptual art by such artists as Donald Judd, Dan Flavin, and Mel Bochner. The impassive gray stucco and sandblasted glass facade conceals a trio of handsomely proportioned, skylit display areas. 341 N. Canon Dr. 310 777 2400

11 Xi'an (1996, Coscia-Day) Spirited interior, with angular cut outs and a temple-like inner dining room; low fat contemporary cuisine—maybe the best Chinese on the Westside. 362 N. Canon Dr. 310 275 3345

12 Nic's (1998, Unruh Boyer Architects) Larry Nicola sold his downtown restaurant and moved west to offer his inventive cuisine in an elegant, comfortable room that opens onto the sidewalk and the Martini lounge next door. 453 N. Canon Dr. 310 550 5707

12 Artistic Eye Michael Sparks designs purist eyewear for individualists, using such materials as bakelite and buffalo horn. 459 N. Canon Dr. 310 278 1810

13 Retail Building (1992, Rockefeller-Hricak) A steel and glass prow points up the delicate zig zag ornament of this renovated stucco block (1930); steel mesh canopies emphasize the storefronts. 460 N. Canon Dr.

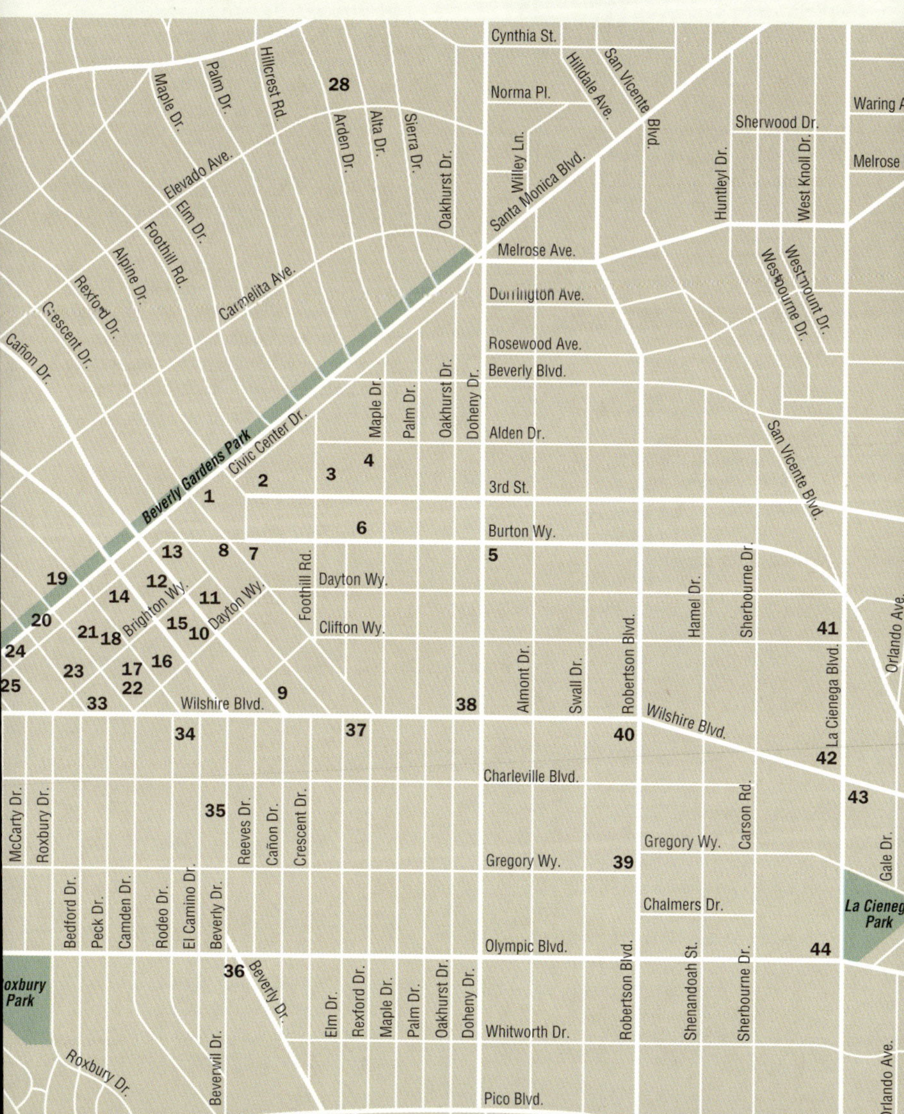

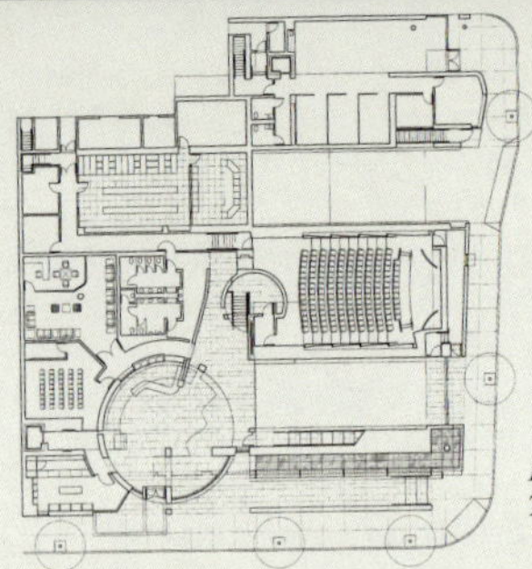

*14 Museum of
Television & Radio*

14 Museum of Television & Radio (1996, Richard Meier & Partners) Pristine white geometry that enhances a major street corner, gives the neighborhood a lift, and welcomes the public to browse its collection of tapes. Whether the contents justify the elegant container is doubtful. 465 N. Beverly Dr. 310 786 1000

15 Anthropologie (1999, Ron Pompeii A.D.) Big-boned timber facade inserted into a glorious bow-truss warehouse that's been scrubbed and allowed to speak for itself. 320 N. Beverly Dr. 310 385 7390

16 Anderton Court (1953-54, Frank Lloyd Wright) Quirky late work, notable for the ramp that ascends around an angular light well past a succession of undistinguished boutiques. 328 N. Rodeo Dr.

17 Gucci (1999, Studio Sofield & Brand + Allen Architects) Monumental stone facade; lofty cubistic interior overlooked by a mezzanine gallery; travertine, white lacquer, and chrome frame the pricey goods. 347 N. Rodeo Dr. 310 278 3451

18 Guess? (1998, Kanner/Roberts with Jonathan Browning of Guess?) Class for a chain: shiny steel I beams frame a glass facade and an open two story space with a sculptural cherrywood stair leading up to the skylit mezzanine. The brushed stainless rails give a sharp, sexy image to the affordable casual wear. 411 N. Rodeo Dr. 310 247 8667

18 Frette Elegant, expensive Italian linens. 449 N. Rodeo Dr. 310 273 8540

19 O'Neill House (1978-88, Don M. Ramos) Writhing stucco swirls and figures, accented with colored tile, evoke Gaudi in this collector's house and rear alley guest house. 507 N. Rodeo Dr.

20 Parking Structure (1989, Maris Peika/Gruen Associates) Split level concrete decks with well-integrated lighting along the south side of N. Santa Monica Blvd, from Linden to Beverly Dr.

21 Gagosian Gallery (1995, Richard Meier & Partners) A roll-up garage door links this soaring white space to the sidewalk; clerestories and a rooftop scoop bathe the interior in natural light. Changing exhibitions of major contemporary artists. 456 N. Camden Dr. 310 271 9400

22 Prego Great pizzas, Italian comfort food, and a lively bar in a handsome room. 362 N. Camden Dr. 310 277 7346

22 Christie's Art and objects are exhibited before auctions; catalogues available from past events. 360 N. Camden Dr. 310 385 2600

23 Medical Building (1990, Jerde Partnership) Three story office block with a well-articulated facade and courtyard, clad in red Indian sandstone to play off its brick neighbors. 436 N. Bedford Dr. 310 273 9880

24 Azia (2000, Coscia Day) The owners of Xi'an have opened this Pan-Asian restaurant in a Japanese-inspired room that features a curved concrete bar and a backdrop of black bamboo. 9601 S. Santa Monica Blvd.

25 Crustacean (1997, Elizabeth An) The owner/designer drew on her Vietnamese heritage for the exceptional seafood cuisine, and for the layout and decor of this elegant restaurant, applying the principles of feng shui to every space and form. The tone is set by the winding, glass-covered koi stream. 9646 S. Santa Monica Blvd. 310 205 8990

26 Café Blanc Elegant, Japanese-inflected cuisine in a cool, minimal storefront. 9777 S. Santa Monica Blvd. 310 888 0108

26 Creative Artists Associates (1989, I.M. Pei/Pei Cobb Freed) Bowed marble, steel and glass facade, and circular lantern give a lift to the corner and symbolize the power of former top agent Michael Ovitz. S. Santa Monica Blvd. at Wilshire Blvd.

27 Spadena House (1921, Henry Oliver) Dream house for a good witch; this steep roofed, shingled fantasy was born as a movie set and office in Culver City, and was moved (on a broomstick?) to this spacious site. Walden Dr. at Carmelita Ave.

28 House (mid 2000, Edward R. Niles) Printed glass screen wall partly conceals the fragmented geometry of this "village of forms, penetrated by sunlight and landscape," as the architect describes it. 710 N. Arden Dr.

29 Familian House (1971, John Lautner) Walls and pyramid constructed of massive rocks, extending a tradition of boulder houses that began a hundred years ago. 1011 Cove Way.

30 Hale House (1949, Craig Ellwood) Delicate exposed steel frame supports thin stucco panels in a house perched above a rustic lane. 9618 Yoakum Dr, right off Benedict Canyon Dr.

31 Frederick Weisman Collection Major collection of 20th century art, brilliantly displayed in a Wallace Neff house, gardens, and **art pavilion** (1991, Franklin D. Israel Design Associates), which is itself a

Black: exterior only, or open to public **Blue:** interior; by appt. only **Red:** private residence, do not disturb **Green:** park, or public open space

work of art, with its reticent Katsura-inspired street facade, and lofty gallery. Individual and group visits by appointment. 275 N. Carolwood Dr, N. of Sunset Blvd. 310 277 5321

32 **House** (1999, Belzberg Architects) A gray metal roof arches gracefully over the bowed, steel-troweled stucco walls of a handsome corner house that is crisp but unthreatening, open yet respectful of its owners' privacy. A gem. 301 S. Linden Dr.

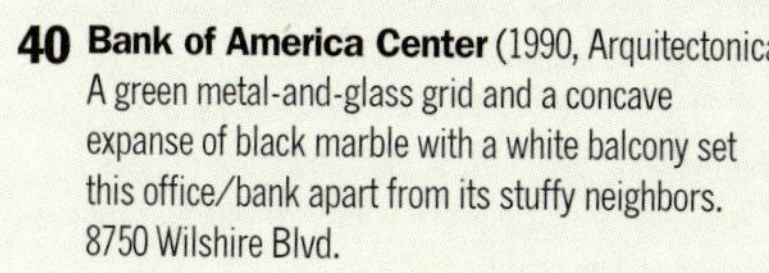

32 House

33 **Sotheby's** Art and objects are exhibited before auctions; catalogues available from past events. 9665 Wilshire Blvd. 310 274 0340

34 **Regent Beverly Wilshire** (1927, Walker & Eisen; new interiors 1990, Glenn Texeira/Project Associates) LA's grandest hotel, admirably remodeled and refurbished. **The Dining Room** is equally handsome and serves very good food. 9500 Wilshire Blvd. 310 275 5200

35 **Dental Cosmetic Center** (1991, Michele Saee) Cutaway curved planes reveal skylights, conceal what lies beyond, and seem to enlarge the confined space. Treatment cubicles fan out like a row of teeth. 241 ½ S. Beverly Dr. 310 276 8537

36 **Avalon Hotel** (1999, Koning Eizenberg; interiors, Kelly Wearstler) Imaginative adaptation of three post-war buildings that preserves their Googie flavor, but brings them up to date in amenities and furnishings. A hip hideaway at a middling price. 9400 Olympic Blvd. 310 277 5221

37 **ICM** (1990, Richard Keating/SOM) Faux facade of limestone panels suspended over a non-loadbearing frame of anodized copper "beams." Behind is a surprisingly urbane entrance courtyard with beguiling water sculptures by Eric Orr. 8942 Wilshire Blvd.

38 **Kate Mantilini** (1987, Morphosis) Hi-tech roadhouse: a complex, layered space within a remodeled curtain-walled bank building. A jagged steel sundial rises from floor to roof lantern; the boxing mural is by John Wehrle. If you stay to eat, stick to basics. 9101 Wilshire Blvd. 310 278 3699

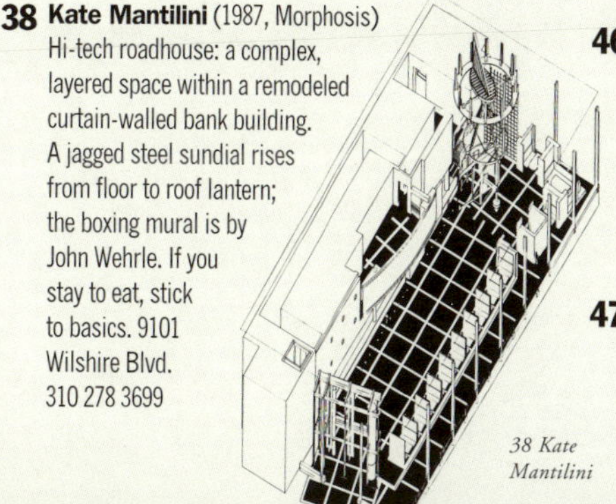

38 Kate Mantilini

39 **Orange** Marne Dupere has picked an eye-catching selection of vintage furniture for home offices. 245 S. Robertson Blvd, at Gregory Way. 310 652 5195

40 **Bank of America Center** (1990, Arquitectonica) A green metal-and-glass grid and a concave expanse of black marble with a white balcony set this office/bank apart from its stuffy neighbors. 8750 Wilshire Blvd.

41 **Le Meridien** (1991, interiors by Frank Mingis; 1996, suites by Zebrowski Design Group) Formerly the Hotel Nikko. Cool, restrained decor, handsomely crafted, with a strong Japanese influence. 465 S. La Cienega Blvd at Clifton Way. 310 247 0400

42 **Matsuhisa** Extraordinary Japanese seafood from an inventive chef, served to serious foodies in a disarmingly plain room. 129 N. La Cienega Blvd. 310 659 9639

43 **Great Western Bank** (1972, William Pereira Associates) A bronze John Wayne rides into the sunset beside this oval glass tower. Wilshire at La Cienega Blvds.

44 **AMPAS Center for Motion Picture Study** (1990, Frances Offenhauser/Michael J. Mekeel/Shin Isozaki) Masterly conversion of the abandoned Beverly Hills waterworks, designed by an engineer who was inspired by the Giralda tower in Seville. Superb library and special collections open to serious researchers. 333 S. La Cienega Blvd. 310 247 3000

Century City

Century City chills the blood. A '60s megablock development of the former Fox back lot, bleak and soulless, with barren plazas and filing cabinets stuffed with lawyers, its only redeeming features are a couple of good towers and a lively outdoor shopping center.

45 **Fox Plaza** (1987, Johnson Fain & Pereira Associates) Iconic 34 story tower, made famous in the movie *Die Hard*, composed of two square shafts rotated and merged, with varied cladding of granite and glass to refract the light. 2121 Ave. of the Stars.

46 **SunAmerica Center** (1990, Johnson Fain & Pereira Associates) Another tower that shows up the dullness of its neighbors. It presents a curved face to the key intersection of Century City, and is clad in different tones of granite and glass to achieve an illusion of depth. A three story arcade around the lobby and pocket park welcome pedestrians. 1999 Ave. of the Stars.

47 **1801 Century Park West** (1997, Barton Myers Assoc) Radical renovation of a 1970 office tower, with new fenestration that relates to Century City and to residential neighbors. Corner of S. Santa Monica Blvd.

Westwood A Mediterranean-inspired shopping village, houses, and apartments were developed around the new UCLA campus by the Janss Company in the late '20s and '30s. The village has lost much of its original character, but still has bits of good period architecture, a dwindling band of quality stores, and some of LA's best movie screens (especially Mann's Village, Bruin and National Theatres).

University of California Los Angeles (UCLA)

Around 55,000 students and staff on one of UC's smallest (419 acres) campuses. Thanks to Campus Architect Charles Oakley and former Dean Richard Weinstein, UCLA has recovered the respect for quality design, long dormant, that inspired George W. Kelham's 1926 master plan and the original core of Romanesque-style brick buildings by Kelham and by Allison & Allison (**Royce Hall**, **Powell Library**, etc). Almost the only exceptions to the mediocrity of the next 55 years were the **University Elementary School** (1948-58, Neutra & Alexander) on Sunset Blvd; the modest **Student Placement & Career Planning Center** (1977, Frank O. Gehry & Associates); the inspired landscaping, which includes some of LA's finest trees; and the **Murphy Sculpture Garden** at the heart of the campus. Over the past decade, Oakley has energetically pursued top talent, and has tried to knit together campus, people and buildings, improving connections. The largest addition in view is the new **UCLA Medical Center** (2004, Pei Partnership), which will replace the congested, earthquake damaged hospital with a luminous, welcoming structure.

Maps and parking tokens can be had from kiosks at each entrance; the free Campus Express buses circulate every five minutes, M-F 7am-6pm. Starting from the SW corner, notable buildings include:

1 **Campus Gateway** (1991, Hodgetts + Fung)
A quiet overture in plain and patterned brick. Le Conte
Ave. at Westwood Blvd.

2 **Medical Plaza: Outpatient Care Center**
(1991, Mitchell Giurgola with DMJM) Mass and
complexity are concealed within a humanely
proportioned, crisply detailed concrete block with a
single-loaded corridor that looks out onto the entrance
court through tall glass bays. **Revlon Breast Care
Center** (1997, Israel Callas Shortridge Associates)
Transformation of an existing basement, offering a
richly layered, intimate interior village in lieu of
a sterile instititution.

3 **Chiller/Cogeneration Plant** (1994, Wes Jones/
Holt Hinshaw Pfau Jones) The campus power hub
puts the machine on a pedestal. An impressive
superstructure of pipes and tanks, gushing steam,
emerge from a patterned brick podium.

4 **MacDonald Medical Research Laboratory**
(1991, Venturi Scott Brown with Payette Associates)
**Gonda (Goldschmied) Neuroscience &
Genetics Research Building** (1998, Venturi Scott
Brown with Lee Burkhart Liu) Two "painted sheds" of
richly patterned brick with fanciful ground level arcades
flank a courtyard set halfway up a slope. Folded glass
planes at the south end of Gonda enclose break-out
areas to promote social interaction among the researchers. On the first floor is **Café Synapse** (1999, Studio
Francesca Garcia-Marques), a stylish self-service
restaurant with whimsical lighting and crisp details.

5 Bradley International Center (1997, Ricardo Legorreta) Steel-framed multipurpose building, clad in the strongly colored stucco that is the architect's signature.

6 Southern Regional Library Facility (1995, Franklin D. Israel Design Associates) Boldly modeled windowless facade, hunkered down into the landscape, masks an expansion of the reserve stacks and new reading rooms.

7 Ackerman Student Union (1996, Rebecca Binder) Muscular addition faced in poured concrete panels, banded with red sandstone; a pergola of glulam beams arches over the roof terrace. It houses a bookstore, lounges, and meeting spaces, which wrap around the old building, enhancing its presence on a major plaza.

8 Powell Library (1927-29, George W. Kelham; restored 1993-96, Moore Ruble Yudell) Tower and facade modeled on San Zeno in Verona; the richly ornamented interior has been sensitively upgraded and extended.

8 Royce Hall (1928-29, Allison & Allison; restored 1994-97, Barton Phelps & Associates and Anshen & Allen) The 2000 seat auditorium is wrapped with classrooms, the reinforced concrete structure is clad in ornamental brick and modeled on Sant' Ambrogio in Milan. This glorious deception has been seismically upgraded, acoustically enhanced, and elegantly refurbished to host the finest performing artists.

9 DeCafé (1997, Dagmar Richter & class) Constructivist lecture/exhibition space and student lounge with spiky steel and plywood fittings and light wands within the concrete shell of the former architecture library. #1302 Perloff Hall.

10 Dickson Art Center Drab brick tower to be transformed (better, rebuilt!) by Richard Meier & Partners. Meanwhile, it houses a notable architecture and art library and the **Center for Digital Arts**, which mounts exhibitions at the adjoining **Wight Gallery**.

11 Corinne A. Seeds University Elementary School Addition (1993, Barton Phelps & Associates) Concrete block and exposed steel, scaled to small children, are used for a new entrance and a flexible two level complex to replace scattered classrooms and mesh harmoniously with the old school buildings.

12 John E. Anderson Graduate School of Management (1994, Harry Cobb/Pei, Cobb, Freed & Partners with Leidenfrost Horowitz Associates) Complex of five stone-banded brick buildings arranged eccentrically around a circular landscaped court with walkways threaded though.

13 Law School Library (addition 1997, Moore Ruble Yudell) A new tower, in the spirit of the old, anchors a busy corner; interior spaces have been reorganized and improved; landscaping by Pamela Burton.

14 Geffen Playhouse Picturesque relic of old Westwood, now managed by UCLA, presents lively repertory. 10886 Le Conte Ave. 310 208 5454

15 Eurochow (1929, Allison & Allison; remodeled 1999, Michael Chow) Theatrical white on white restaurant within the stripped shell of a domed, cathedral-like space that was originally the Janss offices. Chow inserted a mezzanine, Venetian bridge, belvedere, and a wine cellar below a glass floor. Huge fun, and the Italian-Chinese cuisine, initially off course, is improving. 1099 Westwood Blvd. 310 209 0066

16 W Los Angeles (Interior redesigned 1999-2000, Dayna Lee) Starwood Group bought the all-suites Westwood Marquis and re-created it as an oasis of cool, clean-lined sophistication, with a stylish new restaurant and bar. 930 Hilgard Ave. 310 208 8765

17 Italian Cultural Institute Exhibitions and lectures on Italian design, plus rare movies and language classes. 1023 Hilgard Ave. 310 443 3250

18 Flax Art Supplies Two floors of brushes, paints, papers and drafting equipment. 10852 Lindbrook Dr. 310 208 3529

19 Gardens on Glendon Excellent pizza, salads and grills in a Spanish-style brick rotunda. 1139 Glendon Ave. 310 824 1818

20 UCLA at Armand Hammer Museum of Art (1990, Edward Larrabee Barnes) Anne Philbrin has infused new energy into this vibrant arts center, offering provocative exhibitions, live events for all ages, and a good bookstore. In 2002, Michael Maltzan will transform the flawed building, exploiting its courtyard, improving flow, and building out the auditorium. 10889 Wilshire Blvd. 310 443 7000

21 Bel Air Camera Big store offering eclectic stock, professional service, and competitive prices. 10925 Kinross Ave. 310 208 5150

22 Circa 2K Entertainment (1999, Nakao Farrage Architects) Low budget transformation of a '40s dance studio into a film production office. Raw steel and white gypsum planes define six work stations and a central skylit conference room in this masterpiece of spatial geometry. 1067 Gayley Ave. 310 208 2324

23 IN-N-OUT Burger (1997, Kanner Architects) Arresting red, yellow and white fast food restaurant that takes its cues from the company's logo, a switchback arrow, and from a vanished village landmark—the "Googie" style Ships restaurant. 922 Gayley Ave.

24 Sheats Apartments (1949, John Lautner) Curved bays, terraces and steps climbing the hillside only hint at the complex interweaving of eight apartments, each with its own garden. 10901-10919 Strathmore Dr.

Black: exterior only, or open to public **Blue:** interior; by appt. only **Red:** private residence, do not disturb **Green:** park, or public open space

25 Landfair Apartments (1937, Richard Neutra) Linear white stucco block and terraces in pure International Modern style; interiors inventively remodeled as student housing. Landfair Ave. at Ophir Dr.

26 Strathmore Apartments (1937, Richard Neutra) Eight-unit apartment court of silver trimmed, white stucco boxes stacked on a hillside; half Taos Pueblo, half machine in the garden. Charles and Ray Eames lived here in the '40s. 11005-11013 Strathmore Dr.

27 Tischler House (1949, R. M. Schindler) One of the architect's last, most original works: its verticality emphasized by a pitched, blue fiberglass vault. Clerestories in the internal room divisions assure privacy and natural light throughout. 175 Greenfield Ave.

28 The Tower (1988, Murphy/Jahn Associates) Slab set at an angle to a busy corner; faceted ends with flared crowns, and sleek multicolored marble and glass cladding to lighten the bulk. A standout amid its stodgy neighbors. 10940 Wilshire Blvd.

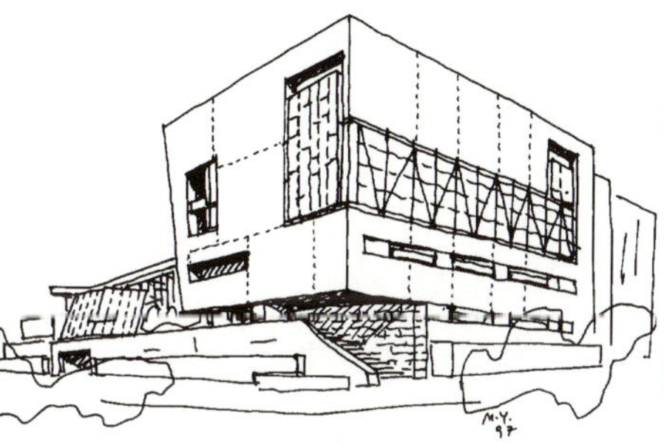

29 Sinai Temple Akiba Academy Expansion

29 Sinai Temple Akiba Academy Expansion (1999, Mehrdad Yazdani/Dworsky Associates) A sculptured five story classroom block, enhanced by a curved wall of Jerusalem stone, holds the main street front, and steps down to a residential scale in back. 10400 Wilshire Blvd. 310 475 6401

30 Lunaria Sophisticated interior, French-Italian bistro cooking, and jazz lounge. 10351 Santa Monica Blvd. 310 282 8870

31 Primi Sleek trattoria serving glorious risotto and grills. 10543 Pico Blvd. 310 475 9235

32 Petal House (1982-84, Eric Owen Moss) Modestly scaled remodel, with a pitched roof that opens like a flower to enclose a hot tub. There's a high level glimpse from the elevated ramp that links the Santa Monica and San Diego freeways—itself one of the great sights of LA. 2828 Midvale Ave.

33 Ove Arup Engineering (1992, interiors by Morphosis) In this remodeled warehouse, exposed steel columns, natural plywood, perforated aluminum, and a polished concrete floor express the elements of the building. An open plan promotes interchange between different disciplines. Glass walled offices and conference room provide privacy where needed. 2440 Sepulveda Blvd. 310 575 4657

34 Absolute Court Reporting (2000, Pugh & Scarpa) A dance rehearsal studio and a training center for court reporters share the core space in this remodeled '40s retail store. The dancers look into the court through a one-way mirror, reversing the usual observer/observed relationship. 11846 Pico Blvd.

35 Studios (1995, J. Staff) Dynamic trio of creative workspaces: a bold mix of cast-in-place concrete and block, with a rounded facing of stainless steel; pylons frame the garage ramp. 2148 Federal Ave. 310 477 9972

36 2117 Fusion fare at bargain prices presented by friendly staff in a minimalist storefront. 2117 Sawtelle Blvd. 310 477 1617

37 Il Moro (1994, Brent Saville) Great pasta and Northern Italian standards in a handsome room or on an enclosed terrace. 11400 W. Olympic Blvd, enter on Purdue Ave. 310 575 3530

38 Architect's Office (1955, A. Quincy Jones; restored 1996, Frederick Fisher & Partners) Built by one talented LA architect for himself, and now occupied by another. Fisher has restored the original freshness of this modest but appealing indoor/outdoor studio. 12248 Santa Monica Blvd. 310 820 6680

39 Raise-Up (1996, Studio Works) Typical LA bungalow, detached from its foundation and raised 16 feet to create a loft space for living, with sleeping areas above. This is an inspiring prototype for expansion on constricted sites, and for the densification that will be needed if LA is not to sprawl halfway to Chicago. 984 Wellesley St.

40 Suissa-Miller Advertising (1996, BAM) Zero-budget remodel of two floors of a white-bread office tower, creating a stimulating workplace for a guerrilla agency. Carpet remnants, concrete block, and industrial hardware are deployed with Brian Murphy's usual wizardry. 11601 Wilshire Blvd, 16th floor. 310 392 9666

41 New York Bagel Company (1990, Frank O. Gehry & Associates) Plywood lined storefront with a skeletal metal Chrysler building slung overhead to stir nostalgia among Big Apple exiles. 11640 San Vicente Blvd. 310 820 1050

42 Donald Bruce Kaufman Branch Library (1994, Arthur Erickson) Privately funded community resource. Two levels are lit from a cylindrical lantern. 11820 San Vicente Blvd. 310 575 8273

42 Vincenti (1997, Osvaldo Maiozzi; interiors, Craig Wright & Judy Stern) In this reincarnation of the legendary Rex il Ristorante, the Milanese cuisine is as refined and pricey, but the cool minimal decor couldn't be more different. 11930 San Vincente Blvd, at Montana-Bundy. 310 207 0127

43 Dutton's Books Abundant selections, with an emphasis on music and literature, plus classical CDs. Expert, friendly service. 11975 San Vicente Blvd. 310 476 6263

43 Del Mano Gallery of Contemporary Crafts Museum-quality glass, ceramics, and lathe-turned wood objects, plus Joseph Shuldiner's lamps. 11981 San Vicente Blvd. 310 476 8508

44 La Mesa Drive Huge Moreton Bay fig trees canopy a street of period-style houses, including notable examples of John Byers' gentle Spanish pastiches of the '20s at # 2021, 2101, and 2153. Enter off San Vicente Blvd.

Sunset Boulevard

An economic and historical cross-section of LA, extending 25 miles from the original settlement to the ocean, passing though midtown grunge and West Hollywood glitz, to become the spine of the affluent residential neighborhoods of Beverly Hills, Bel Air, Brentwood and Pacific Palisades. The first of these lush, winding stretches was immortalized in Billy Wilder's classic movie. Heading west, Sunset becomes even leafier and more serpentine, and though the architecture is generally mediocre, treasures lurk on the side streets amid the expensive dross.

45 UCLA Hannah Carter Japanese Garden (1961, Nagao Sakurai) An idyllic escape; free, but call to make your reservations a month in advance. Tu, W, F, 10am-3pm; groups by arrangement. 10619 Bellagio Rd. 310 825 4574

46 Hotel Bel Air A Mission-style, lushly landscaped retreat from the world, with a fine restaurant, superb service, and prices to match. 701 Stone Canyon Rd. 310 472 5890

47 J.L.M. House (1986, Ted Tokio Tanaka) White hilltop house, inspired by the early villas of Le Corbusier and by traditional Japanese post-and-beam construction. 15210 Antelo Pl, S. of Mulholland Dr.

48 Stephen S. Wise Temple (1968, Dworsky Associates) Sanctuary and fellowship hall in brick and wood: a barn-like building that hugs the landscape. 15500 Stephen S. Wise Dr, off Mulholland Dr. & Casiano Rd. 310 476 8561

49 Skirball Museum & Cultural Center (1996, Moshe Safdie & Associates) A celebration of the Jewish contribution to American life, movingly recounted in the museum, and explored in classes and public programs. Safdie has created a bold concrete frame for these activities in which every room opens onto a courtyard. Coming in 2001-02 are the Ahmanson performing arts complex, a children's heritage gallery, and expanded exhibition galleries. **Zeidler's Café** is open during museum hours for kosher California cuisine. **Audrey's** store (Kanner/ Roberts Architects) is an exemplary build-out. 2701 N. Sepulveda Blvd, at the intersection of the 405 Fwy. & Mulholland Dr. 310 440 4500

Brentwood

50 The Getty Center (1989-97, Richard Meier & Partners) Spectacular views from a hilltop campus that unites architecture, landscape, and art. Meier sought a fusion of permanence and informality, a strong sense of place, and an easy flow of space from indoors to outdoors—notably between the

50 Getty Center

galleries. The buildings, faced in rough-hewn travertine and enameled metal panels, are ranged along two ridges, and interwoven with hard and landscaped open space (by Emmet L. Wemple & Associates and the Olin Partnership). The museum displays sculpture and painting from the Middle Ages through the 19th century, photography, and decorative arts. The complex also includes research and conservation centers, offices, a restaurant and cafeteria, plus an auditorium for public programs. An automated tram links the parking garage at the base of the hill to the arrival plaza. Robert Irwin designed the **Central Garden** as an organic, evolving art work; other commissions

Black: exterior only, or open to public **Blue:** interior; by appt. only **Red:** private residence, do not disturb **Green:** park, or public open space

include a steel sculpture on the plaza by Martin Puryear, a relief in the restaurant by Alexis Smith, and Ed Ruscha's acrylic on canvas in the auditorium lobby. Open Tu-W, 11am-7pm; Th-F, 11am-9pm; Sa-Su, 10am-6pm. 1200 Getty Center Dr, off the 405 Fwy. Information and parking reservations: 310 440 7300

51 Getty South Building (1997, Jeffrey M. Kalban & Associates) Cream stucco maintenance and storage facility tucked into a hillside to protect the sensibilities of its unsightly neighbors, and designed in the spirit of the Meier buildings above. 199 N. Church Lane, backing onto the 405 Fwy.

52 Sand-Mound House (1993, Ted Tokio Tanaka) Another rigorous Corbusian villa in gleaming white stucco. 630 N. Saltair Ave.

53 Sturges House (1940, Frank Lloyd Wright) A broad wood deck is daringly cantilevered from the brick podium rooted in the hillside. John Lautner supervised construction before opening his own practice and must have been as inspired by the task as Schindler was by the Hollyhock House, 20 years before. 449 Skyeway Rd.

54 Schnabel House (1990, Frank O. Gehry & Associates) Seven separate or connected forms comprise a house that achieves a village-like grouping around its front yard, and then drops a story to face back over a canyon. Landscaping by Nancy Goslee Power. 526 Carmelina Ave.

55 Greenberg House (1991, Ricardo Legorreta) Rough yellow and ochre stucco walls, accented by blue-lined slits, enclose a graveled forecourt from which rise vertiginous palms. It's a theatrical prelude to a sequence of dramatic volumes. 223 Carmelina Ave.

Pacific Palisades

56 Kappe House (1967, Raymond Kappe) Concrete towers and laminated beams support the sweeping wood planes of this complex house/studio above a wooded slope. 715 Brooktree Rd. Other notable Kappe houses nearby include 680 Brooktree Rd (1966; delicate post and beam bungalow), 14629 Hilltree Rd. (1969; redwood towers lift the house above a play space), and 596 Dryad Rd. (concrete and steel hillside house).

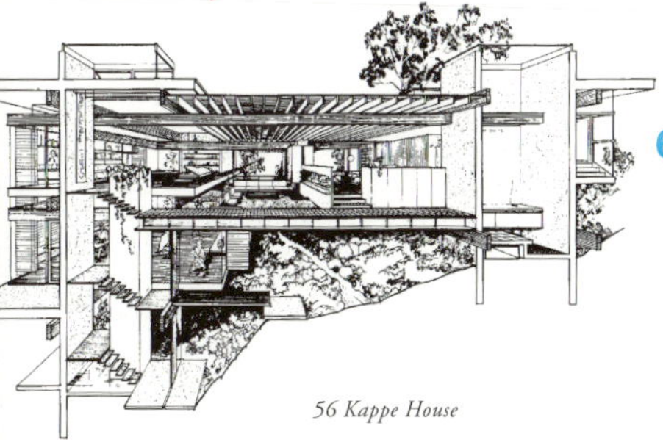

56 Kappe House

57 Silverman House (1995, Rockefeller-Hricak) A streamline cruise ship, with pipe railed decks and a gray stucco facade punctuated with glass brick. 50 Haldeman Rd.

58 Entenza House (1937, H. H. Harris; restored 1997-98, Michael Folonis) Sensuously curved carport and bedroom bay enliven this International Modern house, built for the influential editor of *Arts & Architecture*, and recently turned back to its original condition. 475 Mesa Rd.

59 Worrel House (1926, Robert Stacy-Judd) A chip off the block of the Aztec Hotel (p. 23) giving this enthusiastic proponent of pre-Columbian revival another opportunity to astonish the neighbors. 710 Adelaide Dr.

60 House (1995, Pierre Koenig) From the master of steel, a house that's pared to the essentials: a cube rotated on a base, and screened by a metal and glass fence. 444 Sycamore Rd.

61 Clark House (1997, Melinda Gray) An exploded barn of steel-framed stucco (gray without, boldly colored within) that exploits forced perspective to impart a sense of dynamism. A wood gallery links the upstairs bedrooms and overlooks the lofty living area. 339 Sycamore Rd, off W. Channel Rd.

62 Lederer House (1992, Finn Kappe) Three concrete-block volumes, separated by glazed porches, are ranged along the rim of the canyon. The richly tiled facade of the original 1922 house is incorporated into the street front. 390 Vance St.

63 Eames House (1948-49, Charles & Ray Eames) Poetry and technology combine in this off-the-shelf steel and glass house and studio with their Mondrian-like facades and light filled interiors. It was the most celebrated of the Case Study houses sponsored by John Entenza, editor of *Arts + Architecture* magazine, who commissioned a modest house for himself (now greatly enlarged) from Charles Eames and Eero Saarinen across the meadow. Exterior may be viewed by appointment. 203 Chattauqua Blvd. 310 396 5991

64 Pacific Palisades Gymnasium (2000, Kanner Associates) In this low budget community venture, undulating glass brick and concrete walls wrap around a plain box with oval windows to evoke bouncing balls. 851 Alma Real Dr.

65 Kehillat Israel (1997, Richard Weinstein with Gensler Associates) Rooms are grouped around a central space, opening onto a garden. The sanctuary is inspired by the wooden synagogues of Poland with their ascending roof planes, but traditional themes are given a contemporary spin. 16019 Sunset Blvd. 310 459 2328

66 St. Matthew's Episcopal Church (1982-83, Moore Ruble Yudell) Charles Moore negotiated a consensus amongst the parishioners in designing this joyful celebration of their faith, which speaks to everyone in its mastery of space, play of light, and finely crafted structure. 1030 Bieveneda Ave. 310 454 1358

67 Keeler House (1990, Kappe Architecture) Wooden decks cantilever dramatically from rooms that are stacked against a steep hillside; within, the spaces flow down, through and out. 16525 Akron St.

68 Verrone House (1996, Barbara Bestor with Norman Millar) Wood and stucco family house with flipped roof planes that fuse the client's love of arts and crafts with the architects' devotion to Schindler. 16906 Livorno Dr.

69 Villa Aurora (1927, Mark Daniels; restored 1991-93, Frank Dimster) Hillside Andalusian house, once the home of German emigres Lion and Martha Feuchtwanger, reborn as the California Institute for European-American Relations. Funded by the German Government and City of Berlin (LA's sister city) in memory of the artists who fled to this far shore during the Nazi era. 520 Paseo Miramar. 310 454 4231

70 Sunset Pacific Condominiums (1985, Fitzgibbons Associates) Mixed-use complex of shuttered concrete, with stepped-back terraces and rounded corners, anchoring a key intersection. 17351 Sunset Blvd.

71 Tramonto House/Studio (mid 2000, Cigolle-Coleman) Like the Eames House, this occupies a sloping meadow overlooking the Pacific. The architect couple have rooted their concrete and rough stucco house to the site, and opened it up to the views of ocean, mountains, and walled entry court. 17463 Tramonto Dr.

71 Tramonto House/Studio

72 Rochman House (2000, Israel Callas Shortridge Architects) A '50s house was remodeled and expanded to step down the hillside overlooking the ocean, and conform to strictly enforced height limits. Open plan interiors are cantilevered out and are divided by a central staircase. 17630 Tramonto Dr.

73 Mar Vista Houses (1946-49, Gregory Ain/Ain, Johnson & Day) Easy to imagine you are in Rotterdam, for modernist dreams of affordable, community-oriented housing like this—modest in scale, with shared yards, and inventively planned so that a homemaker had no need of servants—were once denounced as socialistic in the US. Ain was a practical idealist, and many of these 52 flat-roofed houses have been sympathetically extended and cherished. Garrett Eckbo did the landscaping; the trees have grown to dwarf the buildings. 3500 block of Beethoven, Moore & Meier Sts.

74 Vergara House (1999, Daniel Vergara) Inspired by the idea of a "red train running through the existing house," the architect added a 350 sq. ft. studio to the existing Spanish bungalow by cantilevering a colored block out from either side (and thus saving the roots of a camphor tree). 3932 Wade St, Mar Vista.

75 Wildwood Elementary School (2000, Cigolle-Coleman) Zinc-clad classrooms raised on steel columns over the parking lot and linked to the existing building by elevated walkways. Best viewed from Mitchell Ave. 12201 Washington Pl, Mar Vista..

76 Ruppert Photo Studio (1990, Ted Tokio Tanaka) A complex of four studios with oversized representation of a film cassette, peel-off polaroid film and mounting tabs: speaking architecture inspired by Claes Oldenburg. 12130 W. Washington Pl.

Culver City

This early hub of movie making and manufacturing went into a long decline and is now busily reinventing itself. Over the past 15 years, developers Frederick & Laurie Samitaur Smith have commissioned architect Eric Owen Moss to remodel and rebuild a succession of generic bow-truss warehouses, creating signature offices for cutting-edge media companies. This bold development has now achieved critical mass and has spurred many other conversions, transforming the character of the area. In contrast to this new factory town, whose products are images, ideas, and illusions, time seems to have forgotten the century-old residential streets. However, Sussman/Prejza have tried to create a sense of place in this elongated, disjointed community with signs, graphics and "street jewelry" along the main axis of E. Washington Blvd.

77 Steven Ehrlich Office (1999) A 1917 dance hall turned mortuary, which itself died and was boarded up, has been reincarnated as an architect's office, full of light, space and handsome built-ins. 10865 Washington Blvd. 310 838 9700. Across the street is **10950 Studios** (1999, Steven Ehrlich), which ties together two existing buildings to create rental spaces for start-up film companies.

78 Sony Columbia Studios Samuel Goldwyn began this complex in 1916. For 60 years it was home to MGM, which added the PWA moderne **Irving Thalberg Building** (1938, Claude Beelman). You can glimpse this and the stages through the gates; new management has tarted up the old lady, and expanded into the neighborhood. 8336 W. Washington Blvd.

Black: exterior only, or open to public **Blue:** interior; by appt. only **Red:** private residence, do not disturb **Green:** park, or public open space

79 Garden Apartments (1925) The brothers Grimm would have loved this group of shingled cottages and murky pools. 3819-25 Dunn Dr.

80 Tisch-Avnet Offices (1991, Franklin D. Israel Design Associates) Refined yet daring offices for a film production team, housed within an existing four-story building. Steel beams fly through the lobby, stucco walls bend, backlit fiberglass clads a tapered vault in the conference room. 3819 Hughes Ave. 310 838 2500

81 Museum of Jurassic Technology A cabinet of curiosities that's full of surprises and (maybe) a few hoaxes; guaranteed to transport you to a world of wonder. Th, 2-8pm; F-Su, noon-6pm. 9341 Venice Blvd. at Bagley Ave. 310 836 6131

82 Gregg Fleishman Free-form wood furniture by the designer who made his reputation with spring-like ply chairs. By appointment. 3580 Main St, at Culver Blvd. 310 202 6108

83 Culver Studios King Kong roared, Atlanta burned, and boy wonder Orson Welles directed *Citizen Kane* on this lot. Its southern plantation offices were built by pioneer producer Thomas Ince, and used as a trademark by David O. Selznick. 9336 W. Washington Blvd.

84 Keystone Station (1997, Coscia-Day) Culver City's first city hall, sensitively remodeled to house a cafe and book bindery. It's instructive to compare this modest shed to the flamboyant stage set that now houses the municipal bureaucracy, a block west. 3912 Van Buren Pl.

85 Gary Group (1988-90, Eric Owen Moss) For a pace-setting ad agency, Moss transformed two bare boxes into an intricate labyrinth of wood and steel, opening onto skylit courts. The entrance facade is a tilted wall of split concrete blocks; an overlay of chains and steel rebars unifies the side elevation. 9046 Lindblade St, off Ince Blvd. Earlier conversions, including the **Paramount Laundry**, **Lindblade Tower** and **Metafor** adjoin this site. For an appointment to see the interiors of these or other Moss-designed buildings, call Samitaur Constructs: 310 204 4464

86 8522 National Building (1986-90, Eric Owen Moss) Old and new are interwoven in this inventive factory conversion, which ranges a conference room and custom-designed offices for eight adventurous companies along a toplit inner street. 8522 National Blvd. Adjoining this early project are two newer Moss projects: **The Box** (1994) and **Beehive** (2000) both at 8520 National Blvd.

87 Pittard-Sullivan (1998, Eric Owen Moss) To house a leading multimedia digital communications company, Moss broke out of the box of a '30s factory, pushing out four pods to the north, locating the entry in a tilted cylinder, and the second floor conference room in a tilted cube. 3535 Hayden Ave. Across the street are six new and recent Moss projects—a line-up as impressive, though far more varied than the houses on the Rue Mallet Stevens in Paris: **Entertainment Asylum** (1994, 3520 Hayden Ave.), **The Cloud** (1999, # 3524), **Stealth** (2000, # 3530), **Pterodactyl & Parking Garage** (end 2000, # 3540), and **The Umbrella** (2000, # 3542)—a stand out for its cantilvered stepped terrace canopied with slumped glass. This street should be renamed for its architect—or his enlightened patrons.

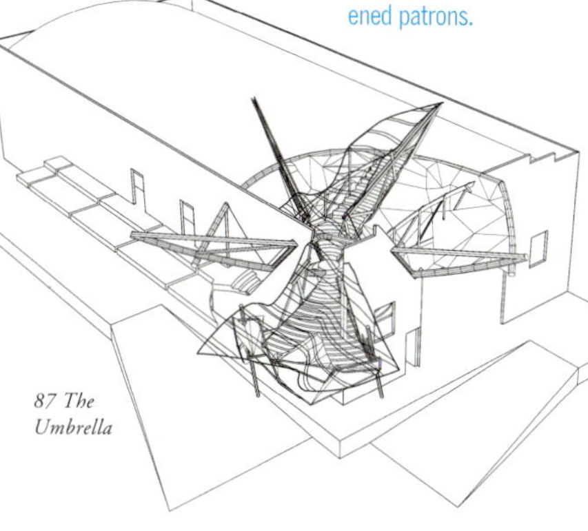

87 The Umbrella

88 Samitaur (1996, Eric Owen Moss) Kodak Digital Design occupies this fusion of new and old, with its boldly expressive exterior staircase, and new block supported on steel legs over an existing road. 3457 La Cienega Blvd. at Corbett St.

89 HSI (2000, Nakao Farrage Architects) To accommodate the complex needs of the world's largest producer of film and video commercials in an existing warehouse, Tom Farrage inserted A frames through the bow-truss vault to draw light into private offices wrapped around a bull pen. A 30 ft. high steel cone provides a fulcrum and canted walls deflect sound and light. 3630 Eastham Dr. 310 452 9999

90 Cool HaRry Exotic, '50s inspired pieces in six sizzling hues and fake fur. An upstairs gallery shows work by like-minded designers. 2734 S. Robertson Blvd. 310 558 2772. Close by is **Harry Art Furniture** which stocks modern furniture of the '20s through the '60s. 8639 Venice Blvd. 310 559 7863

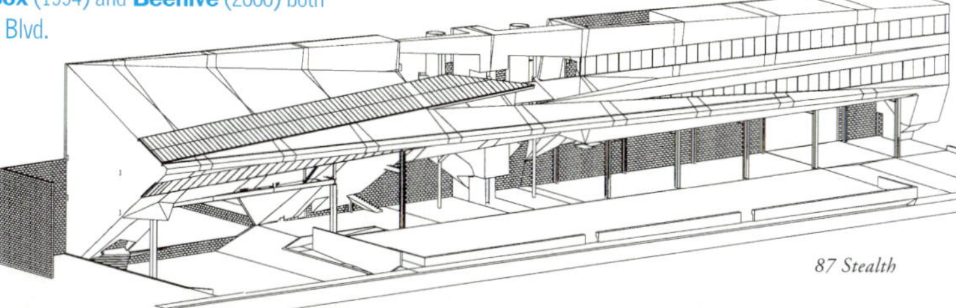

87 Stealth

8 Santa Monica to LAX
San Vicente Blvd.
Georgina Ave.
Carlyle Ave.
14th St.
17th St.
20th St.
20th St.
23rd St.
26th St.
Wellesley Ave.
Centinela Ave.
Berkeley St.
Stanford St.
Nebraska Ave.
Stewart Ave.
Cloverfield Blvd.
Marguerita Ave.
Alta Ave.
Montana Ave.
Idaho Ave.
Washington Ave.
California Ave.
11th St.
9th St.
Lincoln Blvd.
7th St.
4th St.
Ocean Ave.
Palisades Beach Rd.
Wilshire Blvd.
Arizona Ave.
Santa Monica Blvd.
Broadway
Colorado Ave.
Olympic Blvd.
Santa Monica Fwy.
Santa Monica Frwy.
Delaware Ave.
Pico Blvd.
14th St.
11th St.
Pearl St.
20th St.
23rd St.
SANTA MONICA
Santa Monica Municipal Pier
Lincoln Blvd.
Ocean Park Blvd.
Ashland Ave.
Main St.
Ocean Ave.
Barnard Wy.
Pacific Ocean
6th Ave.
4th Ave.
Rose Ave.
Sunset Ave.
Brooks Ave.
Navy St.
Ocean Front Walk
VENICE
Abbot Kinney Blvd.
California Ave.
Palms Blvd.
Speedway
Pacific Ave.
Main St.
Market St.
Grand Blvd.
Windward Ave.
S Venice Blvd.
Venice Pier
N
mi   1/2
Wilshire Blvd.
Arizona Ave.
Santa Monica Blvd.
Broadway
Colorado Ave.
Palisades Beach Rd.
Ocean Ave.
2nd St.
3rd St.
4th St.
5th St.
6th St.
35-49

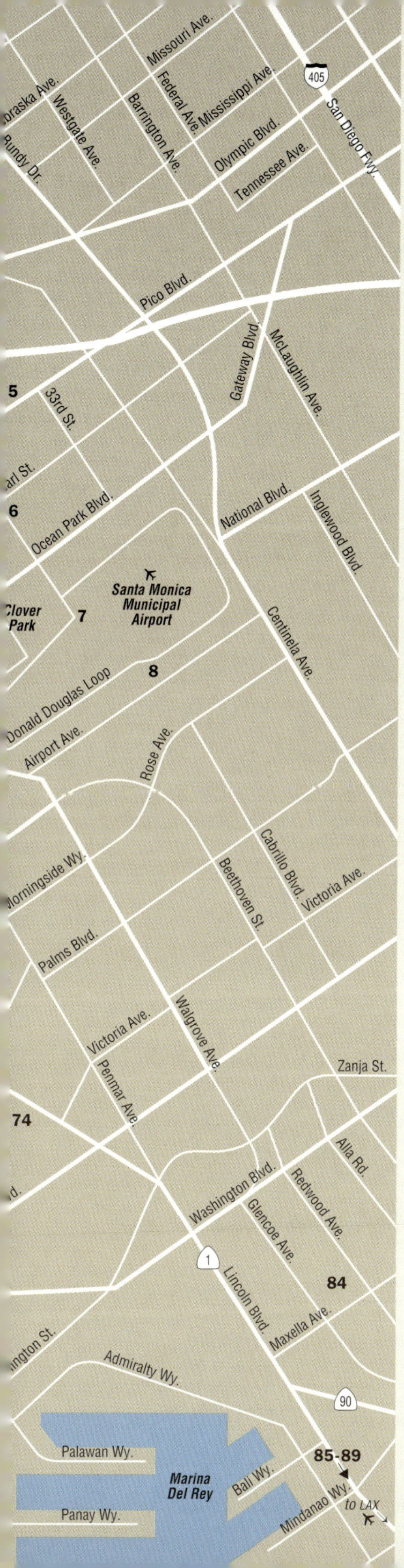

Santa Monica From its modest beginnings as a weekend beach resort, this independent municipality has become a hub for progressive architects, art galleries, and stylish restaurants. Affluent residential neighborhoods contrast with the recycled industrial zone south of Broadway. The city commissioned a new graphic identity program from Sussman/Prejza, and the distinctive blue and yellow street signs, together with a logo inspired by the city seal, evoke sun, sand and ocean—as do their supergraphics on the Big Blue Buses, which are Santa Monica's roving ambassadors to Greater LA.

1   **Garcia Apts** (1993, William Adams) Affordable apartments commissioned by the Community Corporation of Santa Monica. Each block, of seven to nine units, is responsive to its site and has distinctive design features that added little to the minimal construction costs. 1544 Berkeley St. (Also at 1968 19th, 1828 17th, & 1747 7th Sts.)

2   **Blair Graphics** (1999, Randall Stout) A folded canopy of galvanized steel is cantilevered out from a brick shed, and more planes are threaded through to the proofing area of an advanced reprographics company much used by local architects. 1740 Stanford St. 310 829 4621

3   **Syndesis** David Hertz's architectural studio and workshop/showroom for Syndecrete, a strong, lightweight concrete now available in 200 custom colors. Inventive use of scrap materials as ornament. 2908 Colorado Ave. 310 829 9932

4   **Marmol & Radziner Office** Best known for their meticulous restoration of classic Neutra houses (notably the Kaufmann residence in Palm Springs and a project for Gucci's Tom Ford), this prolific design/build firm also does original work. Their airy offices are located in a former chandelier factory. 2902 Nebraska Ave. 310 264 1814

5   **Valentino** Elegant, contemporary setting for the best Italian food and wine in LA—if you order direct from owner Piero Selvaggio and forget the price. 3115 Pico Blvd. 310 829 4313

6   **Suntech Townhomes** (1981, Steve Andre & David Van Hoy/Urban Forms) Three-story houses clustered around walkways atop a podium of parking. The hi-tech imagery has worn well: multicolored stucco, curved stair towers, and stepped-back windows. Pearl at 28th Sts.

7 DC 3 (1989, Solberg & Lowe; interiors by Charles Arnoldi) Spherical entrance and sculptured restrooms anchor either end of this lofty space; a Judd-like wood grid divides it. Planes take off and land from the adjoining runway. Mixed reviews for the California menu. There is a disco next door; the **Museum of Flying** is below. 2800 Donald Douglas Loop N. 310 399 2323

7 Architects' Studio (1997, Regina Pizzinini/Leon Luxemburg/Trygvie Thorsteinsson) A hangar door opens to reveal primary colors defining a two story loft, with an angled blue staircase floating in space. 2828 Donald Douglas Loop N. 310 452 9667

8 The Hump (1998, S.F. Jones Architects) Allied pilots flying supplies to China in WWII called the Himalayas "The Hump." This homage to their daring serves great sushi in a romantic room overlooking Santa Monica Airport. 3221 Donald Douglas Loop S. 310 313 0977

9 Adelman House (1994, Mark Mack) Cubic volumes, delineated by strong color, opening out of each other and defining an outdoor room in back. 619 23rd St.

10 Gehry House (1978/1993, Frank O. Gehry & Associates) This began as a low cost, rough-edged addition of plywood, corrugated metal, and chain-link, wrapped around and interwoven with what the architect called "a dumb little house with charm." Recently extended, softened by Nancy Goslee Power's landscaping, and remodeled within, the house still has the shock of the new. 22nd St. at Washington Ave.

11 Drago (1992, Brent Saville) Stretched vinyl membrane and pierced aluminum tiles absorb sound; Brazilian marble and golden pasta shells etched on glass add color. Celestino Drago's Sicilian specialties highlight the outstanding menu. 2628 Wilshire Blvd. 310 828 1585

12 Koning Eizenberg Architecture (1999, Koning Eizenberg) To demonstrate their ideas on sustainable design, the architects created this energy efficient office, leasing part of the space as artists' studios. 1454 25th St. 310 828 6131

13 MTV Networks West Coast HQ (1997, Felderman & Keatinge Associates) Galvanized steel planes and a projecting red boat transform the facade of an existing office block; plaza and interior (there's an Airstream trailer on astroturf in the lobby) evoke the hip beach life. 26th St. at Colorado Ave. 310 752 8000

14 Bergamot Station (1995, Frederick Fisher & Partners) Fisher masterplanned this conversion of a light industrial complex to create a flourishing center for the visual arts, and designed several individual galleries. Easy parking and physical proximity has turned this venture into a Chelsea west. 2525 Michigan Ave.

Top contemporary art galleries include: **Robert Berman** (310 315 9506); **Patricia Faure** (310 449 1479); **Rosamund Felsen** (310 828 8488); **Bobbie Greenfield** (310 254 0640); **Peter Painter** (310 264 5988); **Shoshana Wayne** (310 451 3773); **Track 16** (310 264 4678). Photography galleries: **Peter Fetterman** (310 453 6463); **Craig Krull** (310 828 6410); **rosegallery** (310 264 8440). Also: **Frank Lloyd** for ceramics (310 264 3866). **Suzanne Felsen** (1998, Koning-Eizenberg; 310 315 1972) and **Sculpture to Wear** (310 829 9960) for exquisite handcrafted costume and semi-precious jewelry. **Hiromi Paper** specializes in handmade papers (310 998 0098). **Art Concepts** does high quality framing (310 315 9772). An anchor for these varied galleries is the **Santa Monica Museum of Modern Art** (1997, Narduli/Grinstein). 310 586 6488

14 Bergamot Station Artists' Lofts (1999, Pugh & Scarpa) A firm that has its own offices at Bergamot and participated in the transformation of the old spaces has designed the first new building: a raw, steel-clad unit of four lofts atop a gallery. A rich collage of materials animates the interiors.

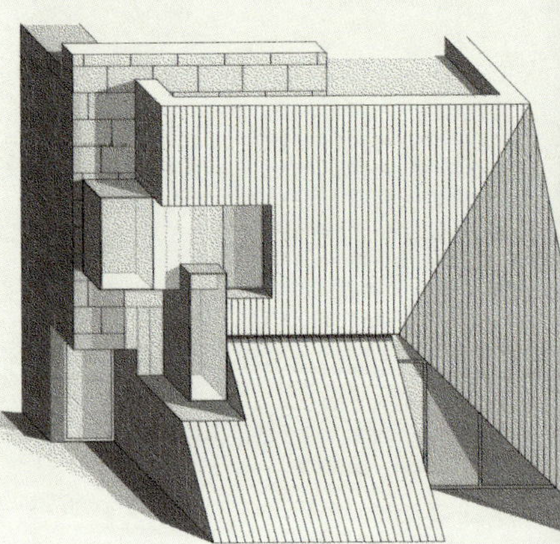

14 Bergamot Station Artists' Lofts

14 Click 3XLA (2000, Pugh & Scarpa) Corrugated steel shed transformed into an interior townscape for a computer animation company. A street flanked by boldly expressed meeting spaces and executive offices concealed by a translucent wall links two plazas. 2415 Michigan Ave. 310 264 5511

15 Crossroads School: Peter Boxenbaum Arts Education Center (1989, Moore Ruble Yudell) Windowless stucco box, with recessed entrance that heralds the central skylit atrium, with two levels of galleries and classrooms opening from it. Another addition to this progressive school is the **Paul Cummins Library** (1996, Steven Ehrlich) which captures its grittiness in a tilted metal roof, exposed steel and concrete block, with bold color accents and inspiring interiors. 1714 21st St. 310 829 7391

Black: exterior only, or open to public **Blue:** interior; by appt. only **Red:** private residence, do not disturb **Green:** park, or public open space

16 Sony Music Entertainment (1992, Steven Ehrlich) Three streamline, sandstone-clad buildings, each with a distinctive lobby, surround a landscaped water court. Offices are ranged around two story skylit atriums. Sculpture gate by Guy Dill. 2100 Colorado Ave. 310 449 2100

17 House (1988-89, Koning Eizenberg) Australian architects building for themselves (with references to homesteads and Glenn Murcutt). The cube in front rotates a few degrees from a bow-vaulted trunk to help enclose the garden/outdoor living room. 1550 18th St.

18 Community Corporation Apartments (1999, Frederick Fisher & Partners) Another demonstration of how committed architects can bring dignity and humanity to affordable housing. Two contextual buildings containing 17 apartments are separated by a courtyard. 1444 16th St.

19 Santa Monica/UCLA Medical Center: Merle Norman Pavilion (1986, BTA) Curved bays of cream stucco with pale green trim evoke art deco apartment buildings, marrying this sophisticated patient care center to the residential neighborhood; interiors open onto terraces and courtyards. 1250 16th St. at Wilshire Blvd. 310 319 4000

20 In-Ex Showroom for witty furniture by owner Ali Alam, plus stylish European imports. 1431B Colorado Ave. 310 393 4948

21 PS #1 Elementary School (1999, Koning Eizenberg Architecture) Child oriented, teacher friendly addition to a private school, comprising seven classrooms, offices, library and multipurpose space. 1454 Euclid St. 310 394 1313

22 Family Service Building (1987, William Adams & Mary Sager) A light filled meeting room, with a delicate facade of Kalwall and glass, rises from a bowed stucco reception area, with consultation rooms leading off a spinal corridor behind. Each role of this non-profit counseling agency has its own expression, but they fit neatly together. 1533 Euclid St.

23 Stiefel & Co. (2000, BAM) Four decrepit warehouses consolidated into a single space for a commercial production company with a village-like interior. At the center is a venting pool, enclosed by pivoting glass doors, which functions as a natural air conditioner. 1620 Euclid St. 310 581 7000

24 Montana Collection (1991, Kanner Architects) Cluster of complementary volumes, solid and transparent, tied together by a rooftop parking deck, reinforce the neighborhood quality of this chic shopping street. Montana Ave. at 14th St. Kanner also designed the steel-braced false front that frames another group of small stores on Montana at 16th St.

24 The Blue House Late 18th and 19th century French furniture and decorative arts. 1402 Montana Ave. 310 451 2243

25 Rosemarie McCaffrey French 18th and 19th century country furniture, especially from Provence, and decorative arts. 1203 Montana Ave. 310 395 7711

26 Freedman House (1978, Raymond Kappe) Cubistic stucco and glass volumes opening off a central stair tower, with a discontinuous steel frame that was originally painted red. 533 9th St.

27 Condominiums (1995, Regina Pizzinini/Leon Luxemburg) Upgraded rental apartments, with new, color modulated facades that recall the geometries of De Stijl. 217 2nd St. (A similar strategy has been employed by the same firm at 519 California Ave.)

28 101 Ocean (Remodeled 1991, Stanley Felderman & Stephen Giannetti) A white ocean liner has run aground, and its rounded stern and gleaming decks are stacked up against the crumbling cliff. Former rental units were converted to luxury condominiums, providing a glittering icon this tawdry strip badly needed. 101 Ocean Ave, N. of San Vicente Blvd.

29 Oceana Suites Hotel (Refurbished 1998, Cheryl Rowley Design) A taste of the Cote d'Azur in this laid back, though pricey, ocean view hotel, with its yellow stucco, vibrant murals, and rattan furniture. 849 Ocean Ave. 310 393 0486, 800 777 0758

30 Windmill Lane Productions (1996, Daly/Genik) Cutting edge commercials and movies are produced in a warehouse that's divided up by wing flaps from B-52s, salvaged from a USAF graveyard in Arizona. The architects and an ad agency share the complex. 1158 10th St. at Colorado Ave. 310 576 1344

31 G. Ray Hawkins Gallery Major source for classic and contemporary photography from California and around the world. 908 Colorado Ave. 310 394 5558

32 Office Building (1999, David Lawrence Gray) Gray designed this new structure as a transition from industrial to residential zones, using concrete block, corrugated steel, and glass to create a play of planes and volumes. A sculptural concrete frame rises from a rock groundscape to define the entry. 1548 9th St.

32 Gray Office Building

33 Club Sugar (1999, John Friedman Alice Kimm) An interior that's as sexy and narcissistic as the kids who dance and make out there; shimmering, reflective planes of translucent plastic pick up the lights within a funky brick warehouse. 814 Broadway. 310 899 1989

34 Santa Monica City Bus Administration (1984, Raymond Kappe & Lotery, Boccato) Streamline office building, clad in blue and white enameled steel panels and raised on pilotis, designed as a symbol of the two block bus yard. It has a major impact from the adjoining freeway. 5th St. at Olympic Blvd.

35 Family Housing (1998, Koning Eizenberg) Another project of the Community Corporation of Santa Monica, mixing townhouses and disabled access units grouped around a common play space. 1128 5th St.

36 JiRaffe Acclaimed French-Californian cuisine in a lofty white room. 502 Santa Monica Blvd. 310 917 6671

37 Reactor Films (1998, Pugh & Scarpa) A cutaway steel container houses the conference room of this free-spirited post production studio. 1330 4th St. 310 656 4646

38 Dormire Francesca Bianchi's pick of high style Italian beds and linens. 1343 4th St. 310 393 9288

38 ICF Authorized importer of Aalto furniture and Unika Vaev fabrics, plus a few new designs. 1345 4th St. 310 659 1387

39 Brightchild (1998, Kanner Architects) A three-dimensional cartoon of bold shapes and sassy colors gives parents as much pleasure as the tots they bring to work off steam. 1415 4th St. 310 393 4844

40 Border Grill (1990, Schweitzer BIM) Rambunctious cantina with punk murals, plus the inventive Mexican food of Susan Feniger and Mary Sue Milliken. 1445 4th St. 310 451 1655

41 Ken Edwards Center (1990, Koning Eizenberg) Services for seniors in a cluster of two story buildings that are scaled to the street and their users. There's a second floor courtyard; parking is concealed below and behind. A model of low cost, responsible building. 1527 4th St.

42 Crew Cuts West (1997, Tierra Sol y Mar) A video editing studio that evokes a sun-filled beach pad with a steel gangplank, knotty pine floors, and louvered shutters. 321 Santa Monica Blvd, 3rd fl. 310 260 0034

3rd Street Promenade Santa Monica Place, a covered mall to the south which Frank Gehry worked on, almost extinguished the old stores along these three blocks. Then the street was landscaped, cars were excluded, and an infusion of movie screens, outdoor cafes, and restaurants revived its fortunes. Success may spoil it, as happened on Melrose Ave. Huge gift/clothing emporia and aimless crowds threaten to overwhelm the small, specialized book-stores that moved here in search of affordable rents.

43 Hennessey & Ingalls (1984, Morphosis) Angular metal facade for the biggest architecture, design and art bookstore in LA. 1254 3rd. 310 458 9074. Across the street is **Arcana**, which specializes in out of print books on art and photography. 1229 3rd. 310 458 1499

43 Johannes Van Tilburg Building (1990, Johannes Van Tilburg & Partners) Mixed-use block inspired by Otto Wagner; a refreshing breeze of modernity amid the post-modern pastiches. The first floor is clad in limestone; the offices above have expansive windows and step back from 3rd; a bowed roof caps the penthouse. 3rd at Arizona Ave. The same architects designed **Janss Court**, four stories of retail and offices, topped by three apartments that are set back behind a broad terrace and disguised as town houses. 3rd at Broadway.

44 Puma Concept Store (1999, Kanner Architects) All-white loft with exposed steel frames, wood ceiling, brick walls, and concrete floors, punched up by a bright red rear wall. 1350 3rd. 310 458 2777

44 UCLA Design Center Changing exhibitions and extension classes in architecture, interior, and environmental design. 1338 3rd. 310 393 4491

45 Remi (1990, Adam Tihany) Cool, civilized room that takes its cue from Venice, though the Italian cuisine ranges far beyond. 1451 3rd. 310 393 6545

45 Broadway Deli (1990, Steven Ehrlich) Food counters, wine store, and dining room are combined to create an urban market place, with an emphasis on Depression moderne forms and materials. Good for basics, but sometimes overcrowded. 1457 3rd at Broadway. 310 451 0616

46 Second Street Center (1994, Frederick Fisher & Partners) Tightly budgeted block of 44 SRO units and shared facilities over commercial space, which respects its neighbors and provides a valuable social service. 1423 2nd St.

47 Office Building (1999, Tierra Sol y Mar) Stainless steel pylons, a glass tile tower, and round, pivoting windows evoke the moderne; artist-designed fountain and terrazzo medallions at the entrance; lively mural in the lobby. 1424 2nd St.

47 Santa Monica International Youth Hostel (1990, Appleton, Melchur & Associates) Reticent 200 bed facility with a glass-walled lobby that wraps around the historic brick Rapp Saloon, which served as the first Santa Monica city hall. 1438 2nd St.

Black: exterior only, or open to public **Blue:** interior; by appt. only **Red:** private residence, do not disturb **Green:** park, or public open space

48 Shangri La Hotel (1940, William E. Foster) Handsome streamline moderne block with ocean views, uninspired decor, and erratic service. 1301 Ocean Ave. 310 394 2791

49 Santa Monica Pier A faint echo of the seaside amusement park that once extended south to Venice. The '20s carousel with its painted steeds reinforces the period flavor. To the south of the pier is **Carousel Park** (1988, Moore Ruble Yudell) with its dragon of river washed boulders. A bicycle trail extends 22 miles south along the beach to Torrance.

50 Santa Monica City Hall (1939, Donald Parkinson & J. M. Estep) PWA moderne with handsome tiled portal. 1685 Main St.

51 Condominiums (1991, Michael Folonis) Sharp-edged collage of metal, wood, and stucco, with curved balconies and boldly expressed chimneys. 830 Bay St.

52 Casa del Mar (Remodeled 1999, Darrel Schmidt Design Associates & Cheryl Rowley Design) Opened in 1926 as an opulent beach club, this Renaissance-style landmark has been transformed into an expensive hotel, with vast public rooms, grand marble staircase, and witty touches in the guest rooms. The **Oceanfront Restaurant** lives up to its name, and offers surprisingly original fare for a hotel. 1910 Ocean Front Walk. 310 581 5533, 800 898 6999

53 Condominiums (1982, Jim Stafford & Rebecca Rinder) Hi-tech imagery enlivens the tightly knit facades; spacious interior volumes. 116 Pacific St.

54 Horatio West Court (1919, Irving Gill) Four units opening off a narrow court: a pristine example of Gill's unique blend of Mission and modern. 140 Hollister Ave.

55 Angles Gallery Steel-troweled stucco box with north-facing skylight; a minimalist setting for adventurous art. 2230 Main St. 310 396 5019

56 Carmen's European Deli (1997, Lorcan O'Herlihy) Sharp-edged remodel of generic mini mall store, employing cantilevered metal canopies and a drop plywood ceiling. 2400 Main St. 310 452 1019

57 Edgemar (1989, Frank O. Gehry & Associates) Abby Sher had the courage to defy conventional wisdom and develop this urbane alternative to cookie-cutter mini malls. 2435 Main St. The lively mix of tenants includes:

57 Form Zero (1996, Andrew Liang) The world's best architectural books and magazines displayed to best advantage, with a gallery to the side. 310 450 0222

57 Rockenwagner (1991, David Kellen) Allusions to southern Germany remind owner/chef Hans Rockenwagner of home; his inventive cuisine is closer to California. A delight to the eye and the palate. 310 399 6504

57 Highlights Elegant display of carefully selected lamps, priced competitively. Many more can be ordered from leading design catalogues. 310 450 5886

57 MOCA Store Satellite of the downtown museum, offering books, cards, and inventive gifts. 2445 Main St. 310 396 9833

58 Kippen Condominiums (1991, William Adams) Four 2 ½ story units clad in stucco and metal to the north, shingles to the south; crisp and spacious within. 2318 2nd St.

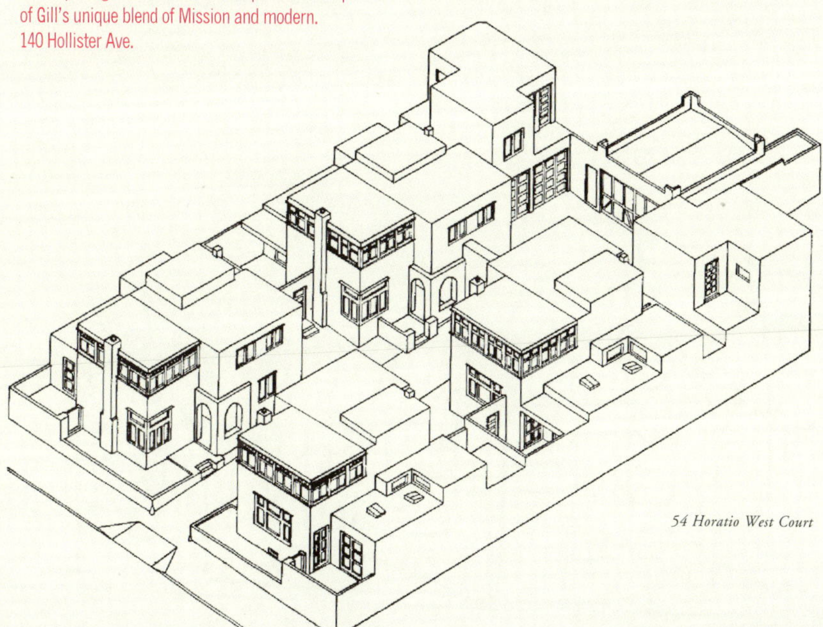

54 Horatio West Court

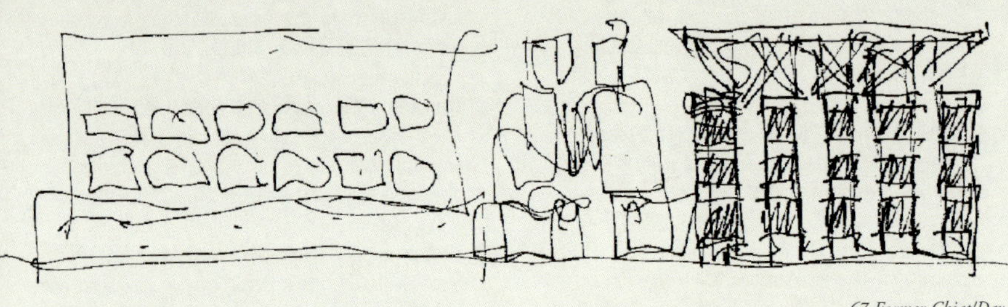

67 Former Chiat/Day

59 Merle Norman Building (1936, George Parr) Streamline office/retail with a nautical flavor, nicely restored. 2521 Main St.

60 Delicatessen R+B (1997, Lorcan O'Herlihy) Crisp white tiled facade and floor (with a nod to the vintage White Castle chain), squares of color (as in a Mondrian), and birchwood built-ins contribute to this appealing eatery. 2645 Main St. 310 396 9095

60 Eames Gallery Changing exhibitions and a good stock of films, books, the House of Cards, and T-shirts that celebrate the legacy of Charles and Ray Eames. 2665 Main St, north of Hill. 310 459 9663

60 Jadis Parke Meek, a veteran of the Eames Office, rents sci-fi props to movie companies in this eye-catching store, but does not encourage casual callers. 2701 Main St. 310 396 3477. Next door is **Paris 1900**, which sells cobweb-fine dresses a century old. 2703 Main St. 310 396 0405

60 Chinois on Main (1985, Barbara Lazaroff) Fellini-esque decor for some of the most dazzling Asian-inspired cuisine in LA. Crowded and very noisy. 2709 Main St. 310 392 9025

61 Library Alehouse (1996, John Hirsch/Hedge Design Collective) A lively play of angles in street canopy and woodsy interior, with a garden in back. 2911 Main St. 310 314 4855

62 Gabbert House (2000, Chu + Gooding) The asymetrical cubes of gray stucco and strategically placed windows are very Schindleresque. 2722 6th St.

63 Armani A/X (1992, Naomi Leff) Within the brick shell of a 1927 Spanish Colonial corner tower, casual wear is displayed in a showroom inspired by army PX stores, Armani's weathered vacation retreat on Pantalleria, and the Maison de Verre. The prototype of what is now a chain of these outlets retains its appeal. 2940 Main St. 310 396 8799

64 Eli Broad Family Foundation (1989, Frederick Fisher & Partners) Brilliantly remodeled, reinforced concrete telephone company building exhibiting part of a contemporary art collection that is made available to museums for exhibition and study. A unique art viewing experience, open Friday afternoons by appointment only. 3355 Barnard Way. 310 399 4004

Venice

Around 1905, tobacco magnate Abbot Kinney drained marshland to create a resort with canals, colonnades, an amusement park, and unfulfilled ambitions to become a center of culture. Storm damage and the discovery of oil soon undid his lofty vision; most of the canals were filled in, and in the '50s, the decrepit buildings lured bikers and beat poets. The renaissance began a decade ago; this quirky, socially mixed area now has some of the most interesting residents and architecture in LA.

Black: exterior only, or open to public   **Blue:** interior; by appt. only   **Red:** private residence, do not disturb   **Green:** park, or public open space

65 Chaya Venice (1988, Grinstein/Daniels) Bronze, copper, natural wood, stone, and a Japanese ceiling mural are combined to achieve a harmonious setting, though the Pan-Asian cuisine and trendy crowd are anything but serene. 110 Navy St. at Main St. 310 396 1179

66 Tangerine (2000, Studio 0.10) A prevoius restoration of this concrete block warehouse admitted more natural light than was wanted by a post-production facility, so the architects' task was to tame and manipulate it, using Therma-Clear channel plastic to diffract it, and fanning white planes in the entry area to open up like flowers to the sun. 221 Rose Ave. 310 450 9700

67 Backyard West (1998, The System Design) An ellipse of drywall separates the private offices and meeting rooms at the periphery from the common areas at the core of this brick warehouse, and a steel stair leads up to a rooftop belvedere to give breathing (and smoking) room to this producer of commercials. 248 Main St, Venice. 310 314 1122

67 Former Chiat/Day (1984-91, Frank O. Gehry & Associates) A major gift to the street: bowed white decks, copper forest, and—as portal and centerpiece—monumental black binoculars by Claes Oldenburg and Coosje van Bruggen. Behind this bold facade are open skylit offices and conference rooms. 340 Main St.

68 Bjornson House (1989, Arata Isozaki) Commissioned by an art collector, this rectangular stucco box with cutaway corners houses a double cube gallery and compressed living quarters. Speedway at Paloma Ave.

69 Studio/Houses (1981, Frank O. Gehry & Associates) Trio of low cost houses for artists, one shingled, one ply-clad, a third in stucco. 322 Indiana Ave.

69 Hopper House (1987-99, BAM) Gabled steel fort on the new frontier, with a white picket fence in front and razor wire in back. The wave form of the roof hints at the spatial drama within, which is constantly evolving. 330 Indiana Ave.

69 John Okulick Studio (1989, Steven Ehrlich) A studio/gallery, 100 ft. long and 32 ft. high with skylit barrel vault supported by red steel bowstring trusses. A luminous space for the viewing of remarkable wood sculptures. 604 Hampton Dr.

70 Joe's Delectable American cuisine and good service in an understated cluster of tiny rooms; book ahead. 1023 Abbot Kinney Blvd. 310 399 5811

70 Ilan Dei "Lush minimalism" is Dei's description of the quirky furniture he makes in his workshop. 1227 Abbot Kinney Blvd. 310 450 0999

71 Electric ArtBlock (1991, Koning Eizenberg) Twenty artists' lofts of varying sizes occupy a linear sequence of five stucco blocks on an abandoned streetcar easement. Crisp detailing and colors on the facades; inventive plans within. 499 Santa Clara Ave.

72 Condominiums (1989, Ted Tokio Tanaka) A geometrical abstraction of a Venetian palazzo. Four units with 18 foot high living rooms behind a glass brick wall and a unified facade of crisp white arches and pediments. 1415 Cabrillo Ave.

73 Studio Building (1993, Lise Matthews & Assoc) Two skylit lofts within a diagonally divided rectangular container of steel-braced concrete blocks. The facade is subtly textured; the cracks in the concrete base were put there before the quake! 1510 Abbot Kinney Blvd. 310 399 7108

74 Villa Superba (1991, John Ruble) A new attic story and conical lantern pop up above the grand pediment Ruble added to his modest bungalow in this street sensitive expansion. 942 Superba Ave.

75 Spiller House (1980, Frank O. Gehry & Associates) Wood frame house and rental unit shoehorned onto a tiny plot. Corrugated steel cladding, woodsy interior. 39 Horizon Ave.

71 Electric ArtBlock

76 William Turner Gallery Specializes in mid-career LA artists, including Charles Arnoldi, Peter Lodado, and David Lloyd. 77 Market St. 310 392 8399

76 72 Market Street (1984, Morphosis) Exceptional American food served in a skylit dining room that opens, through shutters, onto a fragment of the original Venice colonnades; a glass brick wall encloses a back room. 72 Market St. 310 392 8720

77 Windward Circle (1990, Steven Ehrlich) Three lightweight stucco buildings that help enclose the traffic circle (formerly Abbot Kinney's lagoon) and allude to the roller coaster (Race though the Clouds), Antlers Hotel (house/studio), and canal dredge (Ace Market) that could once be seen here.

78 House (1996, David Hertz/Syndesis) A bold house for the architect's family in cement stucco and Douglas fir, with a pergola over the balcony and windows placed to capture views and light. 2420 McKinley Ave. (Syndesis also designed the outwardly inscrutable concrete studio/house at 214 S. Venice Blvd.)

79 LA Louver Gallery (1994, Frederick Fisher & Partners) Tough, complex, luminous spaces in which to see and buy important new American and British art—notably by David Hockney. 55 N. Venice Blvd. 310 822 4955

80 Canals Four restored survivors crossed by humpbacked bridges. Park your car and explore the walkways to the heart of this village-like community. Dell Ave, S. of Venice Blvd.

80 Irani-Beaucage House/Studio (1999, Glen Irani) Crisp two story live/work place for the architect and his wife, a painter, cut away to create a side yard and to open every room to light and air. 419 Linnie Canal Court, fronting on Howland Canal. (Irani also designed the Keck House at 2407 Eastern Canal.)

80 Hess House (2000, Syndesis) Tilt up, insulated concrete walls separated by slits of glass—a fresh spin on Schindler's 1922 studio/house—provides living space for a family on a tiny plot, with rooftop offices for the parents. 477 Carroll Ave. at Eastern Ct.

81 Beach House (1990, Antoine Predock) A model of how to express yourself and achieve privacy on a confined site. Bold concrete frame; expansive windows and roof terrace opening to the beach; translucent side wall. Luminous split-level volumes within. 2315 Ocean Front Walk.

82 Norton House (1984, Frank O. Gehry & Associates) Privacy and complexity on a tiny site, with a log torii for a Japanese-American artist, and a lifeguard shelter for her screenwriter husband. 2509 Ocean Front Walk.

83 Mineries Condominiums (1985, Ted Tokio Tanaka) Gleaming white beach front block with cantilevered balconies on three levels overlooking the ocean and a reticent street facade. 3905 Ocean Front Walk.

84 Ground Zero (1999-2000, Shubin + Donaldson) Twin warehouses—gutted, retrofitted, and linked by a bridge to house a dynamic ad agency. The entry to the main building is at second floor level; from here, a ramp runs the length of the work area past projections of commercials on building-width theatrical scrims. Phase two has curved metal planes and an exposed metal structure carving out volumes within the red brick shell. 4235 Redwood Ave. 310 881 8036

85 Southern California Institute of Architecture Design laboratory established by Raymond Kappe in 1972, as a free spirited alternative to traditional architectural schools. Regular shows of student work and free lectures by top architects in a converted warehouse complex. SCI-Arc will relocate to downtown LA in summer 2001. 5454 Beethoven St. off Jefferson Blvd. 310 574 1123

86 TBWA/Chiat/Day (1998, Clive Wilkinson) An elliptical yellow entry pavilion serves as sign; visitors enter the building by ramps from the second-floor reception as though they were boarding a plane. The 10,000 sq ft. loft has a Main Street lined with stacked container-offices for creative staff, a tree shaded Central Park, bars and basketball hoops, and work stations enveloped in tensile "clouds." Work was never meant to be such fun, but the prize-winning ad campaigns prove that environment does count. 5353 Grosvenor Blvd. off Jefferson Blvd. 310 305 5000

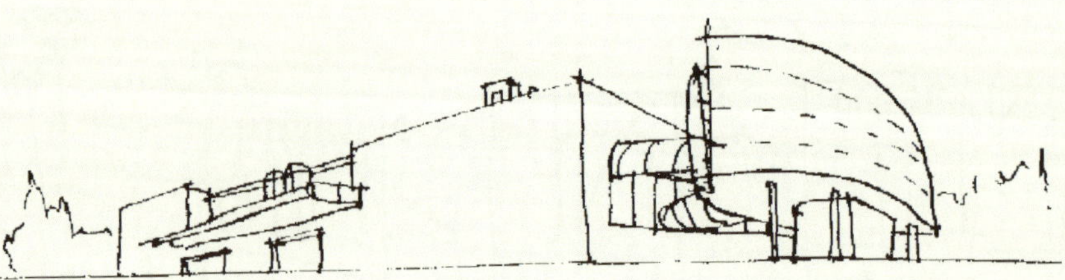

86 TBWA/Chiat/Day

Black: exterior only, or open to public   **Blue:** interior; by appt. only   **Red:** private residence, do not disturb   **Green:** park, or public open space

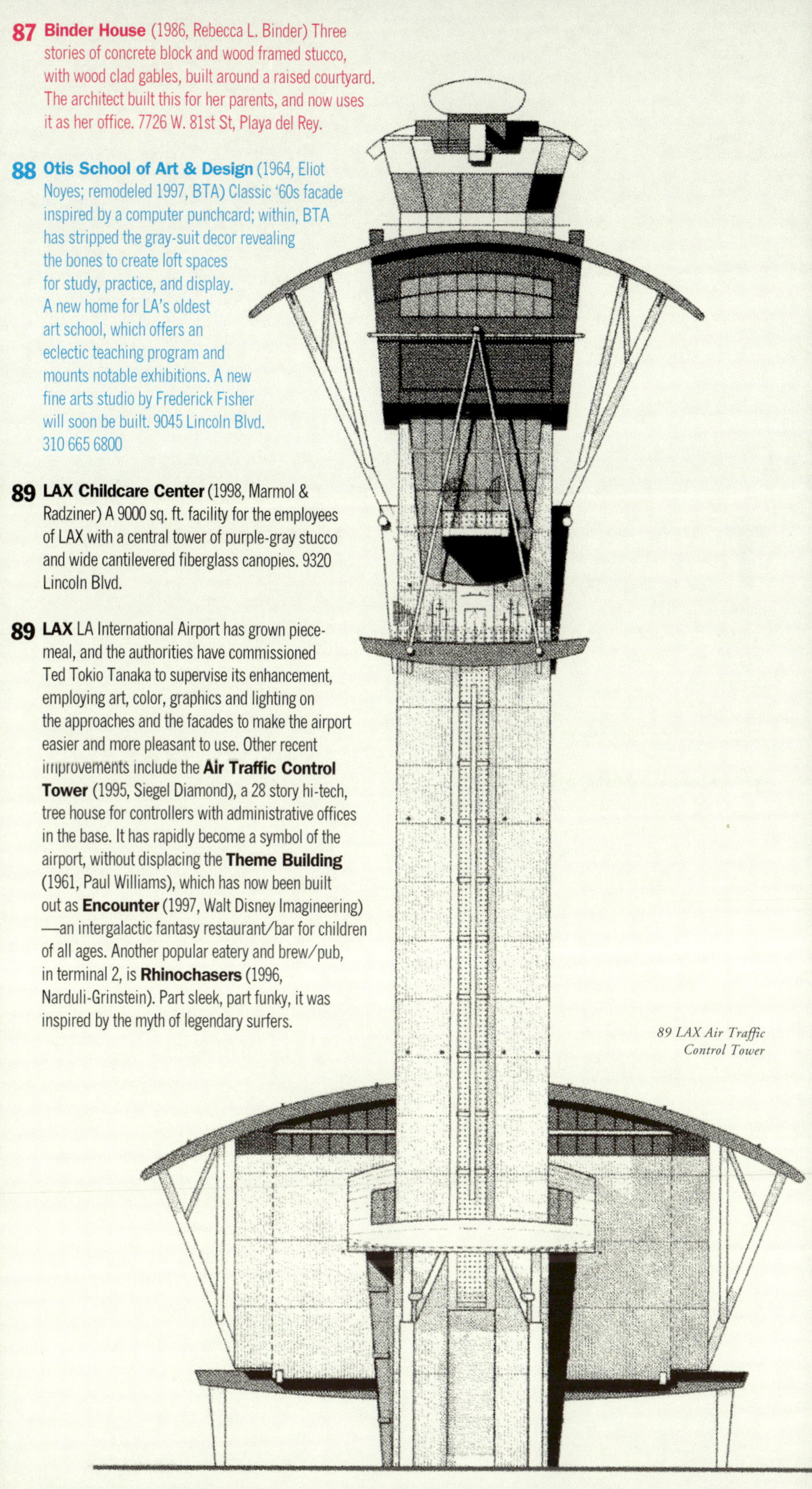

87 Binder House (1986, Rebecca L. Binder) Three stories of concrete block and wood framed stucco, with wood clad gables, built around a raised courtyard. The architect built this for her parents, and now uses it as her office. 7726 W. 81st St, Playa del Rey.

88 Otis School of Art & Design (1964, Eliot Noyes; remodeled 1997, BTA) Classic '60s facade inspired by a computer punchcard; within, BTA has stripped the gray-suit decor revealing the bones to create loft spaces for study, practice, and display. A new home for LA's oldest art school, which offers an eclectic teaching program and mounts notable exhibitions. A new fine arts studio by Frederick Fisher will soon be built. 9045 Lincoln Blvd. 310 665 6800

89 LAX Childcare Center (1998, Marmol & Radziner) A 9000 sq. ft. facility for the employees of LAX with a central tower of purple-gray stucco and wide cantilevered fiberglass canopies. 9320 Lincoln Blvd.

89 LAX LA International Airport has grown piece-meal, and the authorities have commissioned Ted Tokio Tanaka to supervise its enhancement, employing art, color, graphics and lighting on the approaches and the facades to make the airport easier and more pleasant to use. Other recent improvements include the **Air Traffic Control Tower** (1995, Siegel Diamond), a 28 story hi-tech, tree house for controllers with administrative offices in the base. It has rapidly become a symbol of the airport, without displacing the **Theme Building** (1961, Paul Williams), which has now been built out as **Encounter** (1997, Walt Disney Imagineering) —an intergalactic fantasy restaurant/bar for children of all ages. Another popular eatery and brew/pub, in terminal 2, is **Rhinochasers** (1996, Narduli-Grinstein). Part sleek, part funky, it was inspired by the myth of legendary surfers.

This recently incorporated city straggles 20 miles along the Pacific Coast Highway. A few public beaches and points of access interrupt a wall of million-dollar beach shacks. Occasional important beach houses—by such architects as Gwathmey-Siegel, #22350; John Lautner, #22426; Richard Meier, #22466—are largely concealed. Ocean, canyons, and the magical light redeem the seedy commercial strips and the mediocre housing developments on the landward side.

1   **J. Paul Getty Museum** (1972-74, Langdon & Wilson/Stephen Garrett; remodeled and extended 1997-2003, Machado/Silvetti) The pastiche Roman villa, which once held the entire Getty collection, will eventually reopen as a showcase of Greek and Roman antiquities. 17985 Pacific Coast Hwy.

2   **Kappe-Tamuri House** (1996, Finn Kappe & Maureen Tamuri) Powerful steel, glass, and concrete block house, opening up to canyon views: an assertive experiment in creating a lot of living space on a tight budget, and a refreshing change from the self-conscious rusticity of its neighbors. 2255 Topanga Canyon Blvd.

3   **Sternberg House** (1997, BAM) "Tupperware Palladian" is Brian Murphy's description of this cluster of four corrugated plastic pavilions, each containing a separate living zone, protected from the sun by a pitched steel canopy. 2080 Santa Maria Rd. off Topanga Canyon Rd.

4   **Gray House** (1990, David Lawrence Gray) Rigorous poured concrete frame supported on caissons drilled 40 feet into bedrock. The house turns its back on the noisy highway but opens up to the beach, and its interiors have the beauty of a Constructivist tower. 20858 Pacific Coast Hwy.

5   **Waljeski House** (1999, David Lawrence Gray) Steel and concrete house that is fire-resistant, energy efficient, and a strong foil to the rugged landscape of a canyon. Rooms are stacked up the steep slope and open onto cantilevered decks to maximize views. 21160 Las Flores Mesa Rd. off Las Flores Canyon Rd.

6   **McKay House** (1998, Edward R. Niles) Another steel-framed replacement for a house destroyed in a devastating brush fire. Studio, living areas, and master suite are expressed as three Platonic volumes linked by a slotted aluminum deck and supported on columns that penetrate to bedrock. 21757 Castlewood Dr, left off Las Flores Canyon Rd, left on Hume Rd.

7   **Beach House** (1999, Moore Ruble Yudell) An impassive facade of integrally colored, steel-troweled stucco protects this double-lot residence from traffic noise, but one can glimpse the lanterns pushing up from the second story. Three sleeping bays are linked by a deck above the expansive living area. 21348 Pacific Coast Hwy.

3 Sternberg House

Black: exterior only, or open to public   **Blue:** interior; by appt. only   **Red:** private residence, do not disturb   **Green:** park, or public open space

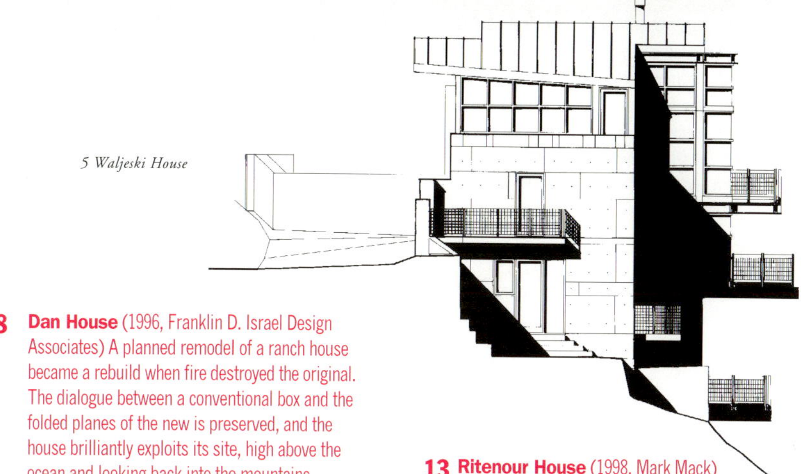

5 Waljeski House

9 **Adamson House** (1928, Stiles O. Clements) Romantic version of an Andalusian farmhouse with colorful Malibu tiles; now a museum. Hourly tours: W-Sa, 11am-2pm. 23200 Pacific Coast Hwy. 310 456 8432

10 **Nobu** (1999, Ralph Gentile, Sophie Harvey) Burnt ash millwork and blood red columns lend distinction to this latest venture by wizard chef Nobu Matsuhisa. Casual dining in an exquisitely detailed, Japanese-inspired interior. 3835 Cross Creek Rd. 310 317 9140

11 **Granita** (1991, Barbara Lazaroff) Whimsical ocean-inspired decor; Puck's signature pizzas and many seafood dishes. 23725 W. Malibu Rd. 310 456 0488

12 **Office Building** (1987, Goldman Firth Associates) Exemplary commercial complex, divided into three two-story buildings with penthouse lofts and pavilions, linked by elevated walkways. The gray-green palette of unpainted plaster, metal and tinted glass, and the drought resistant plantings complement the hills behind. 24955 Pacific Coast Hwy.

14 **Malibu Pavilion** (1990, Edward R. Niles) An urbane complex. Offices occupy a truncated steel-framed, wood-faced cone, opening off a circular court with a central elevator, and facing out over private terraces. 29178 Heathercliff Rd. off Pacific Coast Hwy, west of Kanan Dume Rd. Next door is another Niles original: a stepped wall of offices clad in green tinted glass.

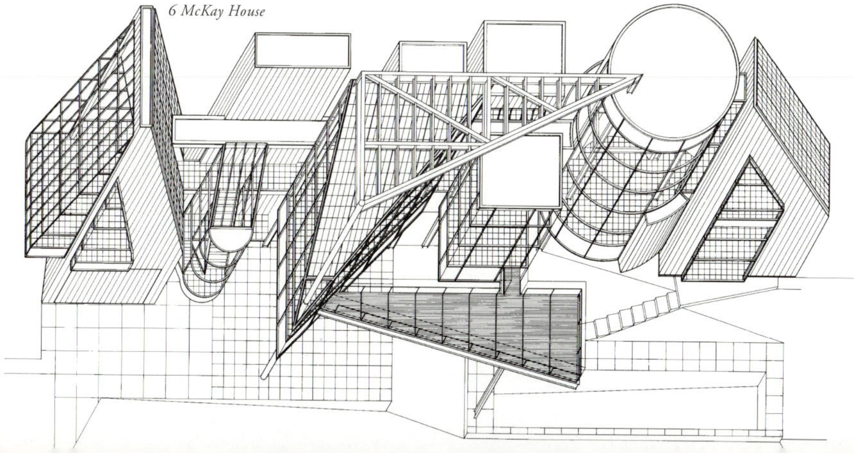

6 McKay House

From El Segundo, with its huge oil refinery and airport related commerce, a succession of tight knit beach communities extends south to the Palos Verdes peninsula, where the real world is held at bay by draconian design guidelines. The coastline turns east and reality reasserts itself in the sprawling port of LA at San Pedro and the industry of Long Beach.

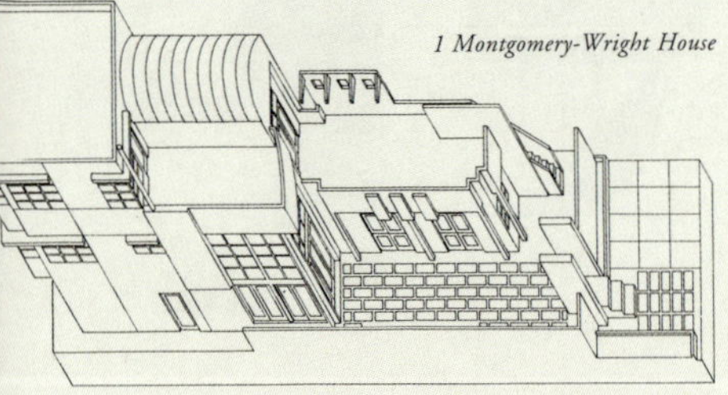

1 Montgomery-Wright House

1 Montgomery-Wright House (1998, Alison Wright) The architect built this three story house for her family, opening it up to the street and side patio by stepping back the upper stories. It's a model of crisp, practical modernism. 437 32nd St, Manhattan Beach.

2 Beach House (1998, Mark Mack) Steel framed remodel of a '50s modern post-and-beam house with a new skin of stained wood and frosted glass enclosing a courtyard on a busy corner site. The interior has been opened up and an apartment added above the garage. 3320 The Strand, Manhattan Beach.

3 Thue House (1996, Rockefeller-Hricak) Wrap around glass for the upstairs living space, looking out to the ocean; sleeping areas tucked into the concrete block base. 3001 Manhattan Ave, Manhattan Beach.

4 Landa House (1996, Morphosis) A canted tower clad in lightweight concrete panels and metal scales rises from the podium of a modest bungalow. The interior of the tower functions as a vertical loft. 328 8th St, Manhattan Beach. A few blocks south is a 1983 house by Morphosis at 3410 Hermosa Ave, Hermosa Beach.

5 Reyna House (1998-99, Dean Nota) Three stories opening up to the beach through canted walls of glass and jutting balconies—a brilliant elaboration of the lifeguard shacks on the sand. 718 The Strand, Manhattan Beach.

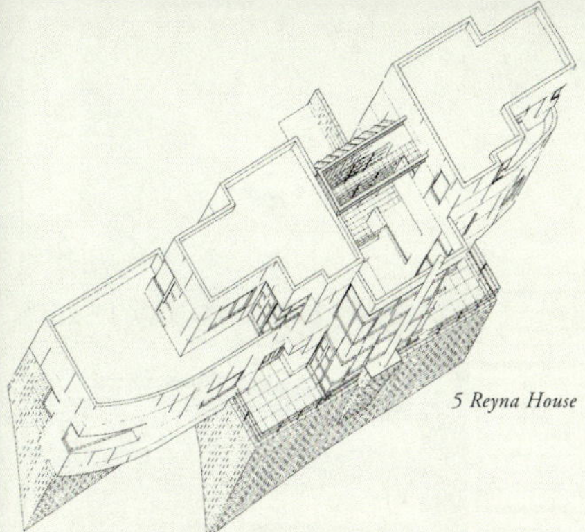

5 Reyna House

6 **Rosenthal House** (1994, Antoine Predock) This steel-trowelled stucco house resembles a cube that has been cut away with an exacto blade, revealing an inner courtyard and exterior stairs, with a concrete pyramid to mark the absent corner. A masterly fusion of visibility and privacy. 606 N. Ardmore Ave, Manhattan Beach.

7 **Elliott House** (1993, Dean Nota) Taut, elegant house that makes the most of a narrow lot, with an elegant metal canopy shading the upper level living spaces, and a conservatory to the north. 2412 Park Ave, Hermosa Beach. A few blocks away is Nota's 1988 **Marsh House**, which exploits a confined triangular plot, evolving from a masonry base to transparent volumes above, with a large central skylight. 2318 Manhattan Ave, Hermosa Beach.

8 **Beach House** (1998-2000, Edward R. Niles) Steel framed, aluminum clad, three story family house with a walled yard and a bowed, stepped plan to maximize views from the second floor living and third floor sleeping areas. 402 The Strand, Hermosa Beach.

9 **Boater's Facility, King's Harbor Marina** (1995, Guthrie & Buresh) Unpretentious shower/locker facility for boaters, designed as a large cabinet floating on an asphalt parking lot. 220 Marina Way, Redondo Beach.

10 **Palos Verdes** A peninsula of great natural beauty, master planned by Olmsted & Olmsted with Charles Cheney in 1922-23 and developed as a "Millionaire's Colony." The merely rich now live there, but the insistence on Spanish style persists. A notable accomodation to this is the **Palos Verdes High School** (1961, Neutra & Alexander) at 600 Cloyden Rd.

11 **Wayfarer's Chapel** (1949, Lloyd Wright) Lyrical wood-framed glass chapel that takes its character from the trees that surround it. 5755 Palos Verdes Dr. S, Rancho Palos Verdes. 310 377 1650

12 **Cabrillo Marine Museum** (1981, Frank O. Gehry & Associates) Village-like cluster of aquarium and other small buildings enclosed in chain link fencing which suggests a playground to the kids who are the target audience. 3720 Stephen White Dr, San Pedro. 310 548 7562. (For whale watching tours, late December-early April, call 310 832 4444.)

13 **Children's Institute International** (1993, Barton Myers Associates) Four nurseries, each in the form of a courtyard house, surround a skylit play area. Second floor library, offices, and meeting rooms are wrapped around this central area, providing visual contact between the staff and the parents and children below. Harbor/UCLA Medical Center, 21810 Normandie Ave, south of Carson Blvd, Carson. 310 783 4677

14 **Signal Hill Golf Center** (1998, Koning Eizenberg) Red painted wood screens and a pro shop checkered like golf socks play off the steel caged driving range and the gritty remains of Signal Hill's once flourishing oil industry. 2550 Orange Ave. 562 492 9555

15 **International Elementary School** (1998, Morphosis with Thomas Blurock Architects) A tough school for a tough neighborhood that compresses the program into half the site that would usually be required and invests the saving in the architecture. In place of strung out little boxes, here is a structure to stretch minds, and a protected rooftop playground. 701 Locust Ave, Long Beach, S. on 710 to 6th St. exit, E. to Locust, turn left.

16 **Queen Mary** Launched in 1934 and moved to moorings here in 1964, the luxury liner that once sailed the Atlantic now serves as a hotel and is open to the public daily, 10am-6pm. Pier J at the end of the Long Beach Fwy. 310 435 3511

11 Wayfarer's Chapel

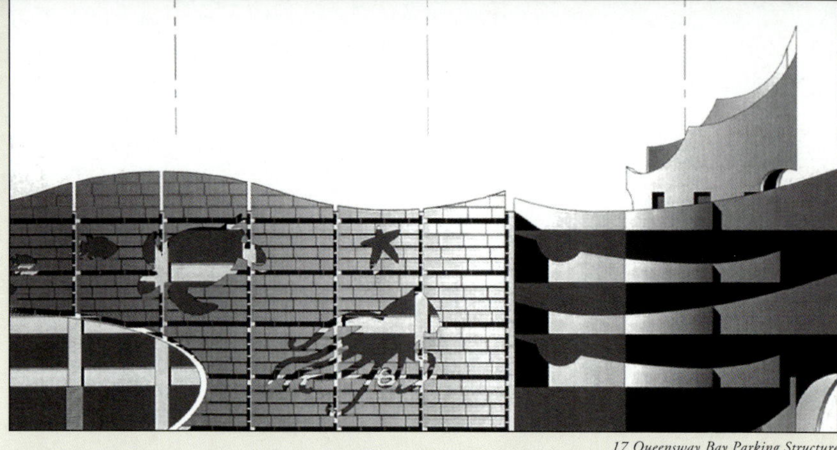

17 Queensway Bay Parking Structure

17 Queensway Bay Parking Structure (1999, Johnson Fain Partners) Bubbles and waves inspired the design of this five story structure, which serves the Aquarium of the Pacific, an IMAX theater, shops, and restaurants that make up Queensway Bay Village. 99 Aquarium Way, Long Beach. Graphics and signage on Queens Promenade by Sussman/Prejza.

18 Long Beach Bikestation (1996, Fernando Vazquez & Peter Carlson) Colorful, lightweight enclosures and a frame that suggests a giant bicycle provide valet parking, changing room, and healthy refreshments for riders taking the Blue Line to downtown LA. A festive amenity, creating a sense of community in a sterile urban development. 1st St. at The Promenade. 310 436 2453

21 Kimpson-Nixon House (1939, Raphael Soriano) Of all the mid-century modernists in southern California, Soriano was perhaps the purest, as this taut, elegant composition shows. Note the delicacy of the entrance canopy. 380 Orlena Ave. off E. Colorado Blvd.

22 Santa Catalina Island Beyond the bustling port of Avalon is wild, undeveloped country, a reminder of what has been built over in LA. Boats leave year-round from San Pedro and Long Beach, making the 26 mile crossing in an hour or so. Visitor information: 310 510 1520

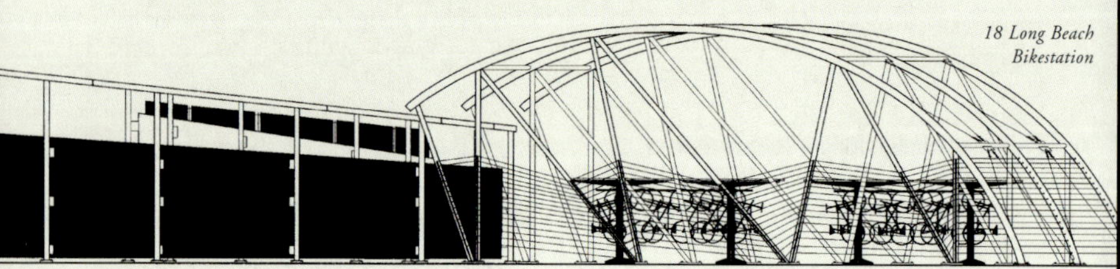

18 Long Beach Bikestation

19 Long Beach Museum of Art (1912; restoration and extension mid 2000, Frederick Fisher & Partners) A new gallery and mixed use structure in the spirit of the existing Arts & Crafts villa, but with a transparent front that draws visitors in and becomes a glowing lantern at night. The carriage house has been remodeled as classrooms and offices. 2300 E. Ocean Blvd. 562 429 2119

20 Raymond House (1918, Irving Gill) Here's consolation for those who mourn the loss of Gill's 1916 Dodge House in West Hollywood: a wonderful proto-modern composition of concrete and hollow tiles. 2724 E. Ocean Blvd.

22 Casino (1928, Webber & Spaulding) Circular Spanish moderne landmark beside Avalon harbor. In summer, movies are shown in the ravishing 1000 seat auditorium with its Art Deco murals, and there's dancing to big bands in the ballroom above.

22 Wolfe House (1928, R. M. Schindler) Dramatic De Stijl tower that exploits the views from this hillside site a short walk from the harbor. 124 Chimes Tower Rd.

Black: exterior only, or open to public   **Blue:** interior; by appt. only   **Red:** private residence, do not disturb   **Green:** park, or public open space

It's a 90 minute drive on the 101 freeway—and a 40 year difference in tempo and style—between LA and Santa Barbara. Founded in 1786 as one of a string of Spanish Missions, it became a fashionable winter resort (together with Pasadena) in the 1890s, and began reinventing itself as a Spanish city following the Panama-California Exposition of 1915. Notable architects produced ambitious plans and the first landmarks; the 1925 earthquake fortuitously removed inappropriate structures. State Street remains a monument to civic vision—though the tourist tide can spoil the magic on summer weekends.

5 **Santa Barbara Museum of Art** (1914, Oscar Wenderoth; remodeled in 1941; additions 1983, 1998) Former U.S. Post Office in Italian Renaissance style; lively exhibitions, plus a good collection of American paintings and ancient sculpture. 1130 State St. 805 963 4364

6 **Santa Barbara County Court House** (1929, William Mooser) If you have time for nothing else in town, see this: a complex of soaring arches, landscaped courtyards and frescoed halls that is one of the triumphs of American historicism. Be sure to explore the interior and climb the tower. 1100 Anacapa St.

1 Plaza de la Guerra, drawing by L. M. Riggs. Courtesy Architecture & Design Collection, University of California Santa Barbara Art Museum

1 **Casa de la Guerra** (1819-26) An early adobe house, restored and used as a historical museum, facing out to a grassy plaza. 15 E. De la Guerra St. 805 966 6961

2 **Meridian Studios** (1923, George Washington Smith) Four artists' studios added to an 1830 adobe with an inner courtyard and north-facing windows. 176 E. De la Guerra St.

3 **El Paseo** (1922-23, James Craig, Mary Craig, Carleton Winslow) To appreciate how difficult it is to attempt historical revivalism today, one has only to contrast this massive, brilliantly planned complex with the Nuevo Paseo across the street: a chain store mall in drag. Beaux Arts architects went to the source; today's rarely do more than mimic the surfaces. 814 State St. Within El Paseo is the **Wine Cask**, a lofty restaurant offering inventive California fare and a great selection of wines. 805 966 9463

4 **Lobero Theatre** (1924, G. W. Smith) Grand symmetrical composition, with steps leading up to an arched portico and a stage tower rising above. 33 E. Canon Perdido.

7 **Christian Science Reading Room** (1951, Kem Weber) A German-born modernist who won acclaim in LA between the wars, and spent his last years in Santa Barbara, building woodsy houses (which are mostly invisible) and designing this streamline moderne gem. 1301 State St. 805 966 4007

8 **Arlington Theater** (1930, Edwards & Plunkett) One of the great "atmospheric" movie palaces converted to use as a performing arts center. It boasts a splendid tower, a paseo leading in from the street, and a backlit Spanish village flanking the auditorium. 1317 State St. 805 963 9503

9 **Mission Santa Barbara** (1812-20) The much restored, oddly flat facade with its engaged columns is exceedingly picturesque. Laguna St. north of Los Olivos.

10 **University of California, Santa Barbara** Established during the post-war boom—an expansive but undistinguished campus with a few saving graces. Architecturally, the standout is the quirky Spanish moderne **Faculty Club** (1968, Moore & Turnbull), now badly in need of restoration. Michael Graves' **Kohn Hall** for the Institute of Theoretical Physics has a notable reading room. Three gilded plaster statues from the facade of the late lamented Art

Deco **Atlantic Richfield Tower** in LA have been re-erected outside the health center. The **University Art Museum**, newly remodeled by Levin & Associates, has a rich and varied collection, and presents important exhibitions. 805 893 8000

10 Architecture & Design Collection The late David Gebhard began acquiring the drawings, correspondence, and models of notable southern California architects, and rapidly built the third largest collection of its kind in the U.S. Highlights include the archives of R. M. Schindler, Irving Gill, George Washington Smith, Lutah Maria Riggs, Kem Weber, Albert Frey, Gregory Ain, and Cliff May. The ADC can be viewed by appointment at the UCSB Art Museum and is currently curated by Kurt G. F. Helfrich. 805 893 2724

Montecito

Tantalizing glimpses of grand estates scattered through the wooded hills, but a few can be visited by appointment, and the beauty of this privileged enclave is compelling. There are even a few modern houses, including those mentioned below and the steel and glass pavilions that Barton Myers built for himself in Toro Canyon.

11 Four Seasons Biltmore (1926, Reginald D. Johnson) The place to stay or to stop by for tea and admire the courtyards, gardens and ocean view. 1260 Channel Dr, Olive Mill exit off the 101 Fwy. 805 969 2261

12 Santa Barbara Cemetery Building (1925, G. W. Smith) Handsome domed chapel. By appointment. E. Cabrillo Blvd at Animas. 805 969 3231

13 Peregrine Galleries Vintage George Jensen and Spratling silver, early 20th century jewelry, and California plein air paintings. Open daily: noon-5:30pm. 1133 Coast Village Rd. 805 969 9673

14 Stewart House (1910, Frank Lloyd Wright) A woodsy Prairie house, direct from Chicago. 196 Hot Springs.

15 Smith House (1920, G. W. Smith) The architect's first house, conveniently close to the road, and a good place to stop and explore, ideally on foot, such neighboring roads as Olive Mill, Oak, and Middle.

16 Lotery House (1997, Rex Lotery) An architect who built modern houses in LA for almost 40 years distilled that experience in this steel-framed hillside house which was designed from the inside out,

taking its form from spaces that soar and flow into each other and reach out for light and views. 920 Camino Viejo Rd.

17 Casa del Herrero (1926, G. W. Smith) The architect's masterpiece, an Andalusian villa full of extraordinary historical fragments and the original owner's inventions; superb garden. Tours by advance reservation. 1387 E. Valley Rd. 805 565 5653

18 Pane e Vino Alfresco salads, pizza and Tuscan fare; a neighborhood favorite. 1482 E. Valley Rd. 805 969 9274

19 Lotusland One of California's most extraordinary gardens, created by Ganna Walska, a failed opera diva, who bought the Cuesta Linda estate in 1941 and worked on it—with help from several leading landscape designers—until her death in 1984 at age 100. Docent led tours: mid Feb. to mid Nov, W-Sa at 10am & 1:30pm. Call M-F, 9am-noon for reservations. Cold Springs Rd. at Sycamore Canyon Rd. 805 969 9990

20 Crawford House (1995, Morphosis) The layered abstract composition of wood, copper, stucco, and finely poured concrete facing the street merely hints at the intellectual rigor and spatial complexity of what lies behind. However, after a surfeit of historicism, this is a bracing sight proving that, even in Montecito,

a few clients have the courage to think differently. 271 Penny Lane. (Equally remarkable is the Blades House by Morphosis, north of Santa Barbara, which is hard to see from the street.)

21 Vedanta Temple (1955, Lutah Maria Riggs) Subtle hints of the Orient and a stunning view. Open to the public. 901 Ladera. 805 969 2903

En route to Santa Barbara, exit the freeway to see:

22 Church of Religious Science (1931, Robert Stacy-Judd) An amazing mix of Mayan and Art Deco in a key building by this eccentric British-born architect. Near SW corner of Santa Clara & Laurel, Ventura. Close by is the **Mayfair Theater** (1941, S. Charles Lee), a streamline moderne bijou movie theater. NW corner of Santa Clara & Ash.

23 California State University, Channel Islands A model mental hospital, built in Spanish style in 1936, will house the first phase of a new campus, master planned by BTA, which is currently remodeling 1.2 million square feet to serve as teaching spaces. New buildings, to be added later, include a library by British architect Norman Foster.

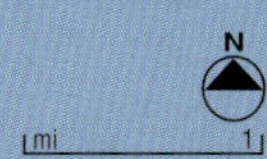

Brace yourself for a boring, smoggy drive of at least two hours on the San Bernardino Fwy. (I-10) through the sprawl of what realtors call the "Inland Empire," which extends far into the desert. For a glimpse of what has been lost, stop off in the idyllic college town of Claremont, and the depleted downtowns of Riverside and Redlands which were once the prosperous hubs of a flourishing citrus industry. In compensation for the blight, a few exceptional new buildings are worth a detour. Try to go between late fall and early spring; the heat is ferocious in summer.

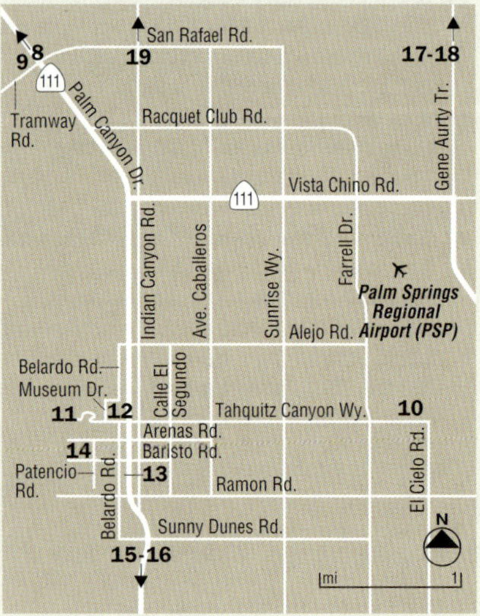

1   California State Polytechnic University, Pomona

California State Polytechnic University, Pomona The sharply angled **CLA Building** (1987-92, Antoine Predock) comprises classrooms, labs and administrative offices and serves as a symbolic gateway to the campus. The College of Environmental Design hopes soon to expand into the fondly remembered **Towell Library** (1991, Hodgetts + Fung), a rough-tech temporary "tent" brought here from UCLA. Exit off 10 Fwy.

2   Diamond Ranch High School (1999, Morphosis) In contrast to their tightly compressed urban school in Long Beach, this high school for 2000 students becomes an extension of the landscape: an escarpment with jutting promontories, and a canyon-like concourse that runs arrow straight through the entire complex. One must experience its complexity, and tours may soon be available. From Pomona Fwy (60) exit at Phillips Ranch Rd, right at off ramp, right to Diamond Ranch Rd. At top of driveway, bear left to parking.

Claremont

Thanks to the Congregationalists who saved Santa Fe's railroad settlement by taking over their failed hotel for a new college, there are now five related colleges, and their spirit is as bucolic as that of a small town campus in the Midwest. Be sure to see the **Pitzer House** (1910, Robert Orr), a boulder clad bungalow at Towne Ave. & Baseline Rd; the **Russian Village**, a Polish immigrant's inspired use of scavenged materials to build a cluster of houses, on South Mills Ave. below Arrow Hwy; and the Churrigueresque **Santa Fe Depot** on 1st St. west of Harvard Ave, from which one might catch a train to Union Station. For a light lunch, there is the **Cafe Harvard Square** at 206 W. Bonita Ave. 909 626 7763

3   Scripps College (1927, Gordon Kaufmann) is described in the Gebhard-Winter guide as one of the prettiest colleges in the country. The **Elizabeth Hubert Malott Commons** (2000, Levin & Associates) is a sensitive expansion of the former Lang Arts Building at Columbia & 10th. **Pomona College** (1887, Ralph Cornell, Myron Hunt) is the oldest and largest of the quintet, and boasts a powerful 1930 mural of Prometheus by the great Mexican artist, Jose Clemente Orozco, in the dining hall. The **Student Center** (1999, Robert Stern) is a felicitous addition of handsomely poured concrete that abstracts the formal language of the older buildings. College Ave. between 2nd and 6th Sts.

4   Arrowhead Regional Medical Center (1999, BTA) From the firm that has lead the way in humanizing hospitals comes this 920,000 sq. ft. medical center in a 90 acre park, built to withstand and respond to the effects of an 8.3 earthquake. Reassuring to know that something will be left standing after the Big One, and encouraging to see how friendly functional architecture can be. Pepper Ave. exit off Fwy. 10 at Colton. 909 580 1000

2 Diamond Ranch High School

Black: exterior only, or open to public   **Blue:** interior; by appt. only   **Red:** private residence, do not disturb   **Green:** park, or public open space

4 Arrowhead Regional Medical Center

Riverside

5 **Mission Inn** (1902-31; restored 1994, ELS)
Overwhelming—imagine San Simeon compressed
into a city block! The chapel has one of the finest
gilded altars outside of Mexico; arched gateways, an
open-air rotunda, antiques, and sumptuous tilework
are reminders of a vanished prosperity. Main, Orange,
6th-7th Sts. 909 784 0300

5 **County Courthouse** (1904, Burnham & Bliesner)
Civic counterpart of the Mission Inn: a Beaux Arts
wedding cake that shows what the public realm once
signified. 4050 Main St.

5 **UCR Museum of Photography** (1990, Stanley
Saitowitz) Brilliant conversion of a former Kress
department store which preserves its Art Deco facade
as a screen and uses the camera as a metaphor to
create a dark chamber that makes the visitor part of
the photographic process. 3824 Main St. 909 784 3686

6 **UCR Fine Arts Seismic Facility**
(1993-late 2000, Israel Callas Shortridge
Associates with Fields & Devereaux)
Annie Chu played a leading role in the
redesign of this ambitious complex, which
will finally be built with Federal funding
for seismic upgrades and repairs. It's
conceived as a gateway to the campus,
and a multilevel, interactive space for art
students that treats roofs as terraces.
University Ave. at Canyon Crest Dr.
909 787 1012

Redlands

7 Architectural highlights include the **Santa Fe
Station** with its Tuscan loggia of 1910, where
passengers once waited for the train (west side of
Orange, south of Pearl); the high Victorian interior of
the **A. K. Smiley Public Library** (SW corner of
Vine & 4th) and the octagonal **Lincoln Shrine** in
back; the elaborate Mission Revival **Holt House** of
1903 (405 W. Olive St.); and the spectacular **Morey
House** of 1890 (140 Teracina, west of downtown).
Many of the old streets have kept their period charm
and grand houses.

Palm Springs

An early hideaway for movie stars blossomed into a
well-watered Eden of golf courses and lavish winter
homes, and finally into another affluent, year round
Sun Belt boom town. Its modernist past has been
rediscovered, celebrated, and is now being marketed
to death. Major houses—by Schindler, Neutra,
Lautner, Ellwood and other local architects—can be
seen only on infrequent architectural tours; however,
one can see several buildings by Albert Frey, a
Swiss-born architect who helped Le Corbusier design
the Villa Savoye, first came to Palm Springs in 1934,
and practiced there until his death in 1998. Recent
buildings are as boringly generic as anywhere else
and the greatest appeal of the city is its proximity to
unspoiled desert and mountains—with an aerial
tramway to carry you aloft.

8 **Desert Hills Premium Outlet Stores** For
those who enjoy Champagne on a Coke budget: great
buys on Prada, Gucci, Barney's, Jhane Barnes, Bose
Electronics, etc. Look for the gas station, **Dinosaurs**
at Cabazon, take the Fields Rd. exit from Fwy. 10, a
few miles before the turn off to Palm Springs. 48650
Seminole Rd. 909 849 6641

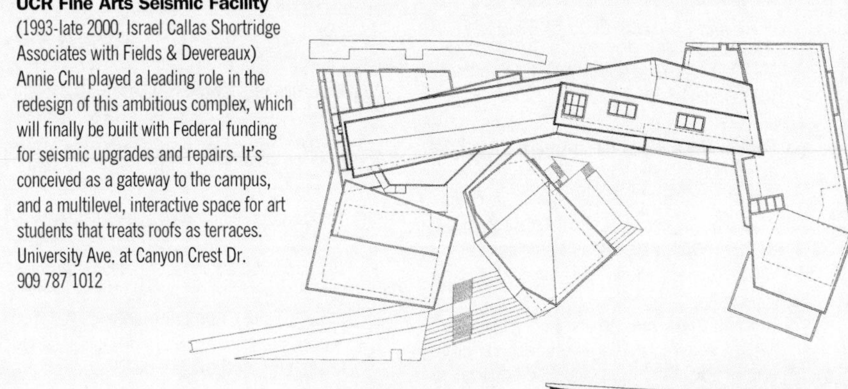

6 UCR Fine Arts Seismic Facility

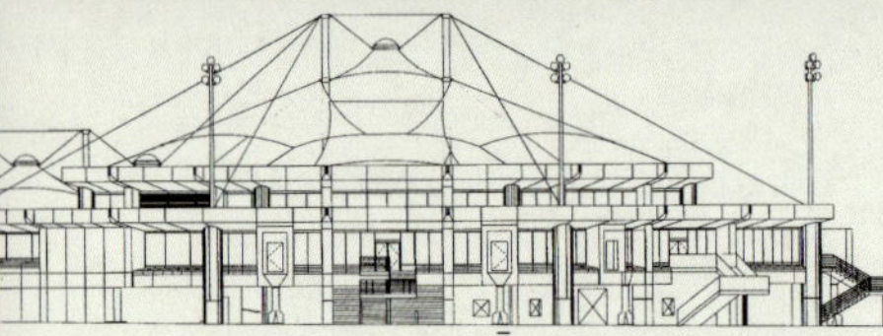

9 Palm Springs Airport

9   **Palm Springs Airport** (Extended 1999, Gensler Associates) All airports grow piecemeal and most lose any character they may once have had. Here's an exception: a teflon-coated fiberglass membrane admits light to the terminal, and passengers can await their flights outdoors in mild weather while enjoying luxuriant landscaping.

10   **Former Tramway Gas Station** (1965, Albert Frey & Robson C. Chambers) The unofficial gatehouse to Palm Springs, now recycled as the **Montana St. Martin Gallery**, and walled in but still retaining its hyberbolic paraboloid roof. 2901 N. Palm Dr. A block away at #2796 is the **Tramway Shell Station** (1964, William F. Cody) with its delicate concrete canopy and oversized bricks.

11   **City Hall** (1952, Frey, Clark & Chambers) Ground hugging concrete block with elegant canopies and steel *brises soleils*; parts of the original have remained unchanged. 3200 E. Tahquitz Canyon Way. Close by at #3111 is the **County Department of Health**, formerly the police station (1958, John Porter Clark), with its double stacked concrete block construction, and at #3255 the **County Courthouse** (1963, Williams, Williams & Williams), which combines elegant steel I beams with concrete block.

12   **Frey House** (1963-64) Perched on a mountain overlooking the city at the end of Palisades Dr. It can be glimpsed from afar, but the street is gated. To request a visit, write to the Frey Fund, PO Box 2310, 101 Museum Dr, Palm Springs, CA 92263.

13   **Palm Springs Desert Museum** (1976-1996, E. Stewart Williams) The city's cultural hub—a reticent cluster of concrete galleries housing a contemporary art collection and temporary exhibitions of growing significance. Concerts in the Annenberg Theatre; sculpture garden and desert trails in back. 101 Museum Dr. 760 325 7186

14   **Former Robinson's Department Store** (1958, Pereira & Luckman) Floating roof and handsome decorative concrete block walls; now Crown Books. 333 S. Palm Canyon Dr. Across the street at #300 is the former **Santa Fe S&L** (1961, E. Stewart Williams), an elegant steel and glass pavilion.

15   **Korakia Pensione** Intimate luxury in a sensitively adapted Moroccan-style villa that a Scottish painter built for himself in 1924. It's achieved cult status, so book far in advance. 257 S. Patencio Rd. 760 864 6411

16   **Chart House Restaurant** (1978, Kendrick Bangs Kellogg) One of that maverick architect's organic structures, which serves basic American fare. 69-934 E. Highway 111, Rancho Mirage. 760 324 5613

17   **The Living Desert** Wildlife and botanical garden that offers a rewarding close-up of plants and critters; hike in winter and take a tram tour in summer. 47-900 Portola Ave, Palm Desert. 760 346 5694

18   To the NE of Palm Springs, a 50 mile loop road runs past the spectacular sandstone formations of **Joshua Tree National Monument**. About 3 ½ miles inside the west entrance is **The Monument** (1990, Schweitzer BIM), a weekend house comprising three skewed pavilions in vivid colors inspired by desert flowers and lichens. Corner of Lobo Pass Rd. & Single Tree Rd.

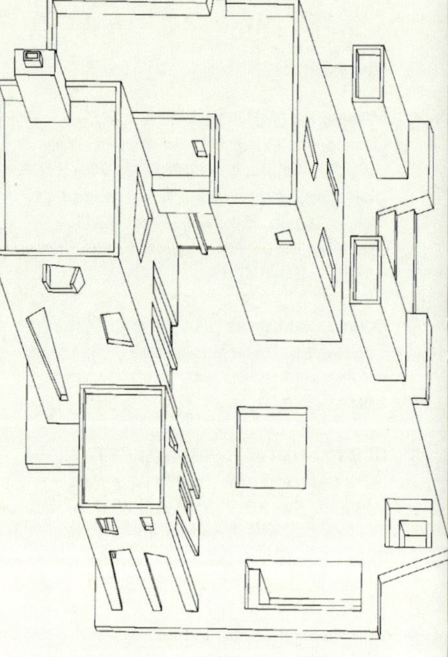

18 The Monument

19   **Institute of Mentalphysics** (1946, Lloyd Wright) Sprawling religious campus inspired by Taliesin West, with buildings by other architects. 59-700 29 Palms Hwy. 760 365 8371

20   To experience Palm Springs as it used to be, Desert Hot Springs offers two intimate places to stay with pools fed by hot mineral springs. **Hope Springs** has ten rooms furnished in '50s style. 68075 Club Circle Dr. 760 329 4003. **Miracle Manor** (1998, RoTo) puts a contemporary spin on a 1948 motel. 12589 Reposo Way. 760 329 6641

Black: exterior only, or open to public   **Blue:** interior; by appt. only   **Red:** private residence, do not disturb   **Green:** park, or public open space

Torrey Pines State Reserve
52
5
1
1
UCSD 2
Genesee Ave.
Eastgate Mall
Miramar Rd.
MIRAMAR
15
Black Mountain Rd.
Escondido Fwy.
US Naval Air Station Miramar
805
Scripps Aquarium Museum
La Jolla Village Dr.
Torrey Pines Rd.
La Jolla Shores Dr.
Torrey Pines Rd.
Gilman Dr.
Regents Rd.
Governor Dr.
163
15
La Jolla Bay
Prospect St.
Torrey Pines Rd.
Ardath Rd.
San Clemente Canyon Park
52
Inland Fwy.
Claremont Mesa Blvd.
3
Pearl St.
Nautilus St.
La Jolla Blvd.
LA JOLLA
La Jolla Scenic Dr.
Soledad Mtn. Rd.
La Jolla Mesa Dr.
Claremont Mesa
Genesee Ave.
Claremont Dr.
Balboa Ave.
Convoy St.
Aero Dr.
Gramercy Dr.
Mission Village Dr.
San Diego Fwy.
274
CLAREMONT
Morena Blvd.
Linda Vista Rd.
Cabrillo Fwy.
Murray Ridge Rd.
Turquois St.
Foothill Blvd.
E Mission Bay Dr.
Lamont St.
PACIFIC BEACH
Grand Ave.
Mission Blvd.
Ingraham St.
Fiesta Bay
Mission Bay Park
LINDA VISTA
Mission Central Rd.
Friars Rd.
Stadium W.
8
Mission Bay
5
Fiesta Island
University of San Diego
163
Ulric St.
MISSION BEACH
Vacation Isle
Sea World
W Mission Bay Dr.
Sea World Dr.
Tecolote Rd.
Friars Rd.
Adams Ave.
San Diego River
Ocean Beach Fwy.
Texas St.
El Cajon Blvd
OCEAN BEACH
8
Sports Arena Blvd.
OLD TOWN
Washington St.
University Ave.
30th St.
Nimitz Blvd.
Chatsworth Blvd.
Lytton St.
Midway Dr.
Pacific Hwy.
Upas St.
Sunset Cliffs Blvd.
Barnett Ave.
San Diego International Airport
1st Ave.
6th Ave.
Park Blvd.
Fern St.
209
Pt. Loma Ave.
Rosecrans St.
N Harbor Dr.
Laurel Ave.
Pacific Hwy.
El Prado
4
Balboa Park
28th St.
Hill St.
Talbot St.
Harbor Island
Ash St.
Broadway
25th St.
31st St.
94
POINT LOMA
San Diego Bay
5
6
Market St.
12th St.
Imperial Ave.
National Ave.
30th St.
32nd St.
Shelter Island
San Diego-Coronado Bay Bridge
Harbor Dr.
5
Pacific Ocean
Cabrillo Memorial Dr.
US Naval Air Station
Orange Ave.
75
CORONADO
7
San Diego Bay
N
Cabrillo National Monument
Silver Strand Blvd.
mi   2

The San Diego Fwy. (405) increasingly resembles a parking lot as early morning and late afternoon traffic grows ever denser, so time your drive with care. Allow a minimum of 2 ½ hours non-stop from West LA to San Diego. In Orange County, Santa Ana, Costa Mesa, Newport Beach and UC Irvine are easily accessible, and the drive gets easier after 405 merges with the I-5 Fwy. The Marines' expansive Camp Pendleton, which flanks Fwy. 5, preserves the rugged landscape that has been built over everywhere else.

Santa Ana

Discovery Science Center (1999, Arquitectonica) A concrete shell was reclad with undulating shadow lines to simulate the strata of the earth and a translucent black cube containing an exhibition space is tilted on one corner to catch the eye of passing motorists. 2500 N. Main St, off Fwy. 5. 949 542 2823

Christy's Donuts (1999, Richard Corsini) Stucco frame, parapet and graphics scaled to the street; part of a city sponsored project to enhance a blighted retail corridor. 1212 S. Bristol St.

Costa Mesa

South Coast Plaza Upscale shopping center serving Orange County's Gold Coast. The design standout is **California Scenario** (1982, Isamu Noguchi), a contemporary Japanese garden of rare beauty. **Rizzoli's Bookstore** is the largest branch outside of New York (714 957 3331). Also of note are **l.a. Eyeworks** and **Mossimo** clothing (1993, Schweitzer BIM). Bristol St, off Fwy. 405. 714 435 2000, 800 782 8888

Pinot Provence (1998, Brantner Design) Brilliant evocation of the south of France (you can almost smell the wild thyme) and delectable cuisine. 686 Anton Blvd, between Bristol & Town Ctr. Dr. 714 444 5900

Gustaf Anders Acclaimed Swedish cuisine and aquavit in a minimalist setting. 3851 Bear St. at Sunflower Ave, S. Coast Plaza Village. 714 668 1737

Outside of the shopping center is the **Orange County Performing Arts Center**, which hosts major artists (714 556 2787). **Plaza Tower** (1991, Cesar Pelli & Associates), is a sophisticated curved structure clad in steel and glass, with double height loggias and setbacks at the 17th and 21st floors.

Newport Beach

Bayside (1999, Peter & Michael Carapetian) Waterfront restaurant/bar that abstracts the Mediterranean vernacular and has a sharp, sensual interior of beeswaxed plaster walls, a baldacchino crafted by a Venetian oar maker, and a fretted steel room divider. Excellent California cuisine. 900 Bayside Dr, McArthur Blvd. off 405. 949 721 1222

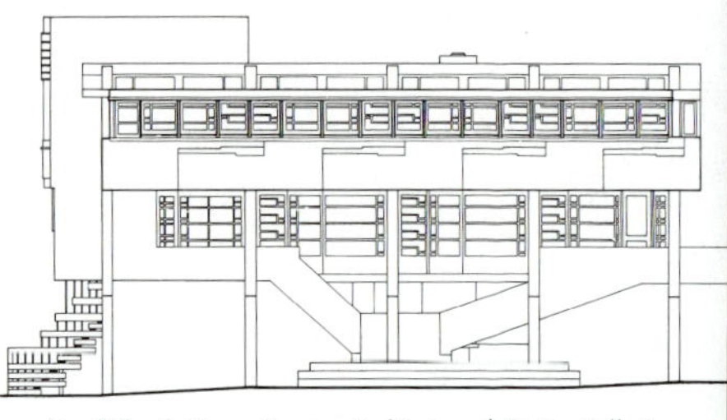

Lovell Beach House. Courtesy Architecture & Design Collection, University of California Santa Barbara Art Museum

Irvine

Arquitectonica is planning a contemporary-style Ritz Carlton. Meanwhile, the only reason to pause here is to see the campus of **UCI** with its science library by Stirling & Wilford, and lesser buildings by Frank Gehry, Morphosis and Eric Moss. Exit Jamboree Rd. from 405, W. to Campus Dr. S. 714 856 5011

San Juan Capistrano

Across from the **Mission**, a picturesque, though touristy ruin, is the **Regional Library** (1983, Michael Graves), a brilliant historical pastiche full of the wit and invention that are missing in his later work. 31495 El Camino Real. Exit 405 on Ortega Highway. 949 493 1752. While you are here, take a look at the Mission-style **Santa Fe Depot** on Verdugo St, a block W. of Camino Capistrano, and the late streamline moderne **Medical Building** at 31866 Camino Capistrano.

San Clemente

Robert Imber founded the **Museum of Architecture** in 1997 to present wide-ranging exhibitions. F-Su, 11am-5pm, or by appointment. Call to confirm new address on Avenida Miramar. Exit 405 on Avenida Palivada, right to El Camino Real. 949 366 9660

Black: exterior only, or open to public   **Blue:** interior; by appt. only   **Red:** private residence, do not disturb   **Green:** park, or public open space

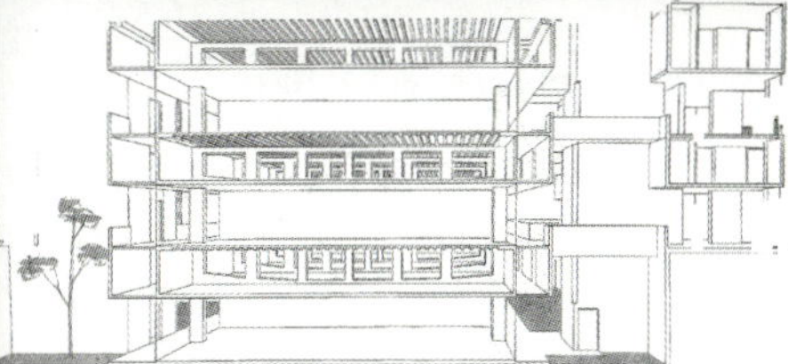

1 Salk Institute

La Jolla

Upscale beach community with an academic bent.
Genesee exit off Fwy. I-5

1 **Salk Institute** (1965, Louis Kahn; additions 1997,
Anshen & Allen) The "architecture of silence and
light" is how Kahn described this symbolic bridge
between the continent and the ocean: a raised
travertine courtyard, bisected by a watercourse and
flanked by poured-concrete research laboratories on
a sawtooth plan. Courtyard open M-F, 8:30am-5pm;
tours by reservation M-F, 11am & noon, noon only on
Th. 10010 N. Torrey Pines Rd. 858 453 4100

1 **Scripps Neurosciences Institute** (1995,
Tsien-Williams with Joseph Wong Associates) Another
scientific monastery of stone and concrete with a
wonderful plaza, but non-monumental in contrast to
nearby Salk. Rather, the architecture is a paradigm
of the human brain, complex and endlessly surprising.
Plaza open weekdays. Interiors may be shown by
appointment. 10640 J. Hopkins Dr. at Torrey Pines Rd.
858 626 2000

2 **UCSD** Expansive, richly landscaped campus
established in 1963; scattered throughout is the
Stuart Collection of contemporary art works—
by Ian Hamilton Finlay, Bruce Nauman, Robert Irwin,
and others. Alexis Smith's path up to Gunnar Birkerts'
overpowering **Central Library** is especially rewarding. Among the buildings, a standout is the **Mandell
Weiss Forum** (1988-91, Antoine Predock), a black
box adjunct of the La Jolla Playhouse that dramatizes
the ceremony of arrival as patrons pass through an
opening in a great mirror, and up a ramp to the
auditorium. Close by are the simple pavillions of
Predock's **Dance Studio** (1997). 858 534 8273

3 **Museum of Contemporary Art** (1998, Venturi
Scott Brown) Gutsy conversion of the house Irving Gill
designed in 1915 for Ellen Browning Scripps, his chief
patron and a generous philanthropist, increasing the
gallery space for a fine collection of California art.
Tu-Sa,10am-5pm; Su, noon-5pm. 700 Prospect St.
858 234 1001

3 A short walk from MOCA are three other notable
examples of how Gill refined and reinterpreted the
Mission style: the **Women's Club** (1913) which
may be visited Sa, 9am-noon. 715 Silverado St. (858
454 2354), the **Bishop's School for Girls**
(1909-16) with additions by others. 7607 La Jolla
Blvd. at Prospect St. (858 459 4021) and **La Jolla
Community Center** (1914). 615 Prospect St.
Two blocks S. of the school, opening off La Jolla Blvd,
is **Pueblo Rivera Courts** (1923, R. M. Schindler),
an experimental housing complex that followed closely
on the architect's own house/studio. 230-48 Gravilla.

San Diego

Once a compact navy town built around its natural
harbor, San Diego has become a sprawling metropolis,
sharply divided between affluent suburbs and a
burgeoning population of aspiring immigrants—
mostly from Mexico, which is a short drive south.

4 **Balboa Park** is one of the largest urban landscapes
in the U.S and boasts its finest zoo, plus picturesque
relics of the 1915 Panama California International
Exposition. Close by is a handsomely restored
conservatory and the **Ford Pavilion** (1936, Walter
Dorwin Teague), a streamline spectacular, highlighted
with neon. The **Museum of Photographic Arts**
presents terrific exhibitions and shows films. 1649
El Prado, Balboa Park. 619 238 7559. Many small
houses by Irving Gill are in Hillcrest on the east side of
the park. These include the Arts and Crafts **Marston
House** (1904, Hebbard and Gill), which is open to the
public F-Su, 10am-4:30pm. 619 298 3142

5 **Horton Plaza** (1988, Jerde Partnership) Pete
Wilson, then an activist mayor, strong-armed a
developer of suburban shopping centers into building
this innovative urban mall as a means of revitalizing
downtown San Diego, which was then on the skids.
Jerde fulfilled this goal by reject-
ing the conventional wisdom of
an enclosed box anchored by
department stores at either
end, and substituting a
picturesque confection
of winding streets,
multilevel decks,
fountains and
loggias, well salted
with references to the
local vernacular, and
enclosed by parking structures. It launched Jerde's
career as an impressario of
colorful urban resorts around the world.

*5 Horton
Plaza*

6 **Children's Museum** Ivan Chermayeff, Zandra
Rhodes, and Lisa Krohn are among the leading
designers who have contributed to "Design Worlds,"
an ongoing series of exhibitions that explain the
principles of architecture and design to small children.
200 W. Island Ave, off Market St, three blocks from
Horton Plaza. 619 233 8792

7 **Hotel del Coronado** (1888, J & M Reid) Built by a
railroad tycoon to be "the talk of the Western World,"
it survives as the last great Victorian resort in
California and one of the largest wooden structures
ever built. Palatial sugar pine and mahogany vaults,
notably in the main lobby and Crown Room. A major
restoration of the interiors and grounds is nearing
completion and tours of the hotel may soon resume.
The Eastlake boat house is also remarkable. 1500
Orange Ave. 619 435 6611

Antique Dealers

Brenda Antin*
7319 Beverly Blvd, LA 323 934 8451

Barokh Antiques*
8481 Melrose Pl, W. Hollywood 323 655 2771

The Blue House*
1402 Montana Ave, Santa Monica 310 451 2243

Circa 1910*
7206 Melrose Ave, W. Hollywood 323 965 1910

Bruce Graney*
1 W. California Blvd, Pasadena 626 449 9547

Anne Hauk*
458 N. Robertson Blvd, W. Hollywood 310 659 3606

Hollyhock*
214 N. Larchmont Blvd, Hancock Park 323 931 3400

Charles Jacobsen*
Pacific Design Center (trade only) 310 652 11878

Japanache*
146 N. Robertson Blvd, W. Hollywood 310 657 0155

Robert Kuo*
8686 Melrose Ave, W. Hollywood 310 855 1555

La Brea Antique Collection*
334 N. La Brea Ave, LA 323 938 9444

Lief*
8922 Beverly Blvd, LA 310 550 8118

Rosemarie McCaffrey*
1203 Montana Ave, Santa Monica 310 395 7711

Peregrine Galleries*
1133 Coast Village Rd, Montecito 805 969 9673

Primary Source (by appointment)
4847 W. Jefferson Blvd, LA 323 732 6131

Warisan*
7470 Beverly Blvd, LA 323 938 3960

Architectural Photographers

Tom Bonner 310 396 7125

Benny Chan Fotoworks 310 449 0026

Grey Crawford 310 558 1100

Douglas Hill 323 660 0681

John Linden 310 301 4023

Grant Mudford 213 663 9888

Stephen Oxenbury 310 471 1284

Erhard Pfeiffer 310 452 0096

Tim Street Porter 323 874 4278

Jeremy Samuelson 323 937 5964

Dominique Vorillon 323 660 5883

Architectural Remnants

Arte de Mexico*
5356 Riverton Ave, N. Hollywood 818 769 5090

European Reclamation*
4524 Brazil St, LA 818 241 2152

Scavengers Paradise*
5453 Satsuma Ave, N. Hollywood 323 877 7945

Architectural Tours & Lectures

AIA/LA*
Pacific Design Center 310 785 1809

Architours 323 294 5825

Chamber Music in Historic Sites 310 954 4300

Googie Tours ('50s strip architecture) . . .323 980 3480

LACMA Decorative Arts Council 323 857 6528

LA Conservancy 213 623 2489

Masters of Architecture (Lecture series)
. . . . .310 785 1808 ext. 20

Neighborhood Place Project 626 448 4022

Pasadena Heritage 626 441 6333

Society of Architectural Historians . .800 972 4722

Southern California Institute of Architecture*
. . . . .310 574 1123

SCI-Arc Children's Architectural Workshop
. . . . .323 655 4028

UCLA Department of Art & Architecture
. . . . .310 825 7858

UCLA Extension (Architectural study tours)
. . . . .310 825 9061

USC School of Architecture 213 740 2723

Venice Art Walk (Artists's lofts & homes in late May)
. . . . .310 392 9255

Woodbury University School of Architecture
. . . . .818 767 0888 ext. 330

Art Appraisals

Jacqueline Silverman
619 N. Almont Dr, W. Hollywood 310 277 4410

Art Conservators

Conservation of Paintings
1660 Stanford St, Studio B, Santa Monica .310 453 7717

Linda Shaffer (works on paper)
1706 S. Genesee, LA 323 936 9112

Tatyana M. Thompson (paintings)
1453B 14th St, Santa Monica 310 451 4135

Art Galleries

Ace Contemporary Exhibitions*
5514 Wilshire Blvd, LA 323 935 4411

Acme*
6150 Wilshire Blvd, LA 323 857 5942

Angles*
2230 Main St, Santa Monica 310 396 5019

Robert Berman*
Bergamot Station, Santa Monica 310 315 9506

Chacmool*
8920 Melrose Ave, W. Hollywood 310 550 6792

China Art Objects*
933 Chung King Rd, LA 213 613 0384

Patricia Faure*
Bergamot Station 310 449 1479

Rosamund Felsen*
Bergamot Station 310 828 8488

Marc Foxx*
6150 Wilshire Blvd, LA 323 857 5571

Gagosian*
456 N. Camden Dr, Beverly Hills 310 271 9400

Gemini GEL*
8365 Melrose Ave, W. Hollywood 323 651 0513

Grant Selwyn Fine Art*
341 N. Canon Drive, Beverly Hills 310 777 2400

Bobby Greenfield Gallery*
Bergamot Station 310 264 0640

Kiyo Higashi*
8332 Melrose Ave, W. Hollywood 323 655 2482

Koplin*
462 N. Robertson Blvd, W. Hollywood 310 657 9843

Margo Leavin*
812 N. Robertson Ave, W. Hollywood 310 273 0603

Karyn Lovegrove*
6150 Wilshire Blvd, LA 323 525 1755

LA Louver*
55 N. Venice Blvd, Venice 310 822 4955

Mendenhall Gallery*
41 Fair Oaks Ave, Pasadena 626 792 0162

Newspace*
5241 Melrose Ave, LA 323 469 9353

Regen Projects*
629 N. Almont Dr, W. Hollywood 310 276 5424

Remba*
462 N. Robertson Blvd, W. Hollywood 310 657 1101

Manny Silverman*
619 N. Almont Dr, W. Hollywood 310 659 8256

Richard Telles*
7380 Beverly Blvd, LA 323 965 5578

William Turner*
77 Market St, Venice 310 392 8399

Shoshana Wayne*
Bergamot Station 310 453 7535

Art Installation, Storage & Shipping

LA Packing & Crating
5722 Jefferson Blvd, LA 323 937 2669

Mark Ross/Smart Installations
1918 N. Main St, #101, LA 323 227 5609

Art Supplies

Flax*
10852 Lindbrook Dr, Westwood 310 208 3529

Pearl*
1250 S. La Cienega Blvd, LA 310 854 4900

World Supply*
3425 W. Cahuenga Blvd, LA .323 851 1350, 800 399 6753

Associations

American Institute of Architects*
Pacific Design Center 310 785 1809

American Society of Interior Design
Pacific Design Center 310 659 8998

Antique Dealers Association of California
(List of LA members) 415 398 8115

International Interior Design Association
Pacific Design Center 310 657 0244

Set Decorators Society of America
Pacific Design Center 310 289 1959

Auction Houses

Butterfield & Butterfield
7601 Sunset Blvd, LA 323 850 7500

Christie's*
360 N. Camden Dr, Beverly Hills 310 385 2600

LA Modern Auctions*
8057 Beverly Blvd, LA 323 904 1950

Sotheby's*
9665 Wilshire Blvd, Beverly Hills 310 274 0340

Blinds

Aero Shade Company (problem solving)
8404 W. 3rd St, LA 323 655 2411

Charles Minne (trade only)
Pacific Design Center 310 659 2466

Window Blind Connection (Competitive prices)
. . . . .800 479 6300

Books: Architecture, Art & Design

Arcana* (out of print)
1229 3rd St. Promenade, Santa Monica . . .310 458 1499

Form Zero*
2435 Main St, Santa Monica 310 450 0222

Gamble House*
4 Westmoreland Pl, Pasadena 626 793 3334

J. Paul Getty Museum*
1200 Getty Center Dr, Brentwood 310 440 7300

Hennessey & Ingalls*
1254 3rd St. Promenade, Santa Monica . . .310 458 9074

LA County Museum of Art*
5905 Wilshire Blvd, LA 323 857 6111

MOCA Store*
2445 Main St, Santa Monica 310 396 9833

Museum of Contemporary Art*
250 S. Grand Ave, LA 213 621 2766

Norton Simon Museum*
411 W. Colorado Blvd, Pasadena 626 449 6840

Rizzoli (also Santa Monica & Costa Mesa)
9501 Wilshire Blvd, Beverly Hills 310 278 2247

UCLA/Hammer Museum*
10889 Wilshire Blvd, Westwood 310 443 7000

Vroman's Museum Books*
340 S. Lake Blvd, Pasadena 626 396 1670

Building Materials

Anawalt Lumber (chain)
11060 Pico Blvd, Westwood 310 478 0324

Home Depot (chain)
5600 W. Sunset Blvd, Hollywood 323 461 3303

House of Moldings
15202 Oxnard St, Van Nuys 818 781 5300

* included in this guide

Cabinetry

Blue Ribbon
640 S. Grand Ave, #107, Santa Ana 714 667 3167

407*
407 S. Fairfax Ave, LA 323 525 1718

Hieronymus Woodwork 310 588 7553

Ceramics, Glass & Crafts

Algabar*
920 N. La Cienega Blvd, W. Hollywood 310 360 3500

Area*
605 N. La Brea Ave, LA 323 934 8474

Art Wares*
8625 Melrose Ave, W. Hollywood 310 652 6428

Craft & Folk Art Museum*
5800 Wilshire Blvd, LA 323 937 5544

Del Mano*
11981 San Vicente Blvd, Brentwood 310 476 8508

Denny Burt*
7208 Melrose Ave, W. Hollywood 323 965 1910

The Folk Tree*
199 & 217 S. Fair Oaks Dr, Pasadena 626 793 4828

Freehand*
8413 W. 3rd St, LA 323 685 2607

Otto Heino (ceramics studio)
971 McAndrew Rd, Ojai 805 646 3393

Po Shun Leong (architectural fantasies)
8546 Oso Ave, Winnetka 818 341 1559

Frank Lloyd*
Bergamot Station, Santa Monica 310 264 3866

Mineo Mizuno (ceramics & sculpture)
2960 Glenmanor Rd, LA 323 660 2449

OK*
8303 Third St, LA 323 653 3501

Retro*
524 ½ N. La Brea Ave, LA 323 936 5261

Shelter*
7920 Beverly Blvd, LA 323 937 3222

Joseph Shuldiner (paper lamps)
5833 Eucalyptus Lane, LA 323 258 5715

Sonnies*
1007 Fair Oaks Ave, S. Pasadena 626 799 8764

Zipper*
8316 W. 3rd St, LA 323 951 0620

Eyeglasses & Jewelery

Artistic Eye*
459 N. Canon Dr, Beverly Hills 310 278 1810

Domont*
8661 Sunset Blvd, W. Hollywood. 310 289 9500

Suzanne Felsen*
Bergamot Station, Santa Monica 310 315 1972

l.a.Eyeworks*
7407 Melrose Ave, W. Hollywood 323 653 8255

Cynthia Leight*
123 S. Robertson Blvd, LA 310 858 7399

Oliver Peoples*
8642 Sunset Blvd, W. Hollywood 310 657 2553

Optical Store of Aspen*
7580 Melrose Ave, W. Hollywood 323 653 5238

Sculpture to Wear*
Bergamot Station 310 829 9960

Traction*
1643 N. Las Palmas, Hollywood 323 463 3700

Fabrics

Bradbury Collection* (trade only)
Pacific Design Center 310 657 3940

Diamond Fabric* (discount)
611 S. La Brea Ave, LA 323 931 8148

Donghia* (trade only)
Pacific Design Center 310 657 6060

International Silks & Woolens*
8347 Beverly Blvd, LA 323 653 6453

Kneedler Fauchere* (trade only)
Pacific Design Center 310 855 1313

Lincoln Fabrics (discount)
1600 Lincoln Blvd, Venice 310 396 5724

Oakmont* (trade only)
Pacific Design Center 310 659 1423

Randolph & Hein* (trade only)
Pacific Design Center 310 855 1222

Scalamandre* (trade only)
Pacific Design Center 310 657 8154

F. Schumacher* (trade only)
Pacific Design Center 310 652 5353

J. Robert Scott* (trade only)
8727 Melrose Ave, W. Hollywood. 310 659 4910

Silk Trading Co*
360 S. La Brea Ave, LA 323 954 9280

Fashion

agnes b*
100 N. Robertson Blvd 310 271 9643

Liza Bruce*
7977 Melrose Ave, W. Hollywood 323 655 5012

Decades & Decades Two*
8214 Melrose Ave, W. Hollywood 323 655 0223

Andrew Dibben*
1618 Silver Lake Blvd, Silver Lake 323 662 9189

kbond Central*
7257 Beverly Blvd, LA 323 939 9779

Peter Lai*
2571 Mission St, San Marino 626 799 4645

Maxfield*
8825 Melrose Ave, W. Hollywood 310 274 8800

Fred Segal*
8100 Melrose Ave, W. Hollywood 323 651 4129
6500 Broadway, Santa Monica 310 393 2322

Tyler Trafficante*
7290 Beverly Blvd, LA 323 931 9678

Faux Painters

Landmark Painted Design & Restoration
624 E. Foothill Blvd, Pasadena 626 359 6113

Real Illusion
1104 Palms Blvd, Venice 310 452 0237

Floor Coverings

Decorative Carpets*
8900 Melrose Ave, W. Hollywood 310 859 6330

Melrose Discount Carpets
7951 Melrose Ave, W. Hollywood 323 653 4653

Pashgian Bros*
993 E. Colorado Blvd, Pasadena 626 796 7888

Stark Carpets* (trade only)
Pacific Design Center 310 657 8275

Furniture, Custom

Ali Acerol
2900 Airport Ave, Unit D, Santa Monica . . .310 915 5100

Jenny Armit*
8210 Melrose Ave, W. Hollywood 323 782 9173

Bruce Bolander (built-ins)
2710 Las Flores Canyon Rd, Malibu 310 456 6719

City Studio*
8444 Melrose Ave, W. Hollywood 323 658 6354

Cool HaRry*
2734 S. Robertson Blvd, LA 310 558 2772

Ilan Dei*
1227 Abbot Kinney Blvd, Venice 310 450 0999

Dialogica*
8820 Beverly Blvd, LA 310 888 0008

Domestic Furniture*
6150 Wilshire Blvd, LA 323 936 8206

Gregg Fleischman (by appointment)
3850 Main St, Culver City 310 202 6108

In-Ex*
1431 B Colorado Ave, Santa Monica 310 393 4948

In House*
7370 Beverly Blvd, LA 323 931 4420

Ipekijian Woodwork (Craftsman; by appointment)
768 N. Fair Oaks Ave, Pasadena 626 792 5025

James Jennings
8471 Melrose Ave, W. Hollywood 323 655 7823

Kids' Studio (uncloying children's furniture)
. . . . .323 655 4028

Madport
18 E. Holly St, Pasadena 626 792 5597

Sam Maloof (by appointment) 909 987 2805

Mark Newman Studios 800 871 7701

Joyce Ortner (also gold & silver leafing)
Santa Barbara 805 683 3406

Pieces*
8280 Melrose Ave, W. Hollywood 323 653 0808

ReForm*
800 Traction Ave, #20, LA 213 680 3010

Jay Reynolds (by appointment) 310 559 6722

Charles Robbins
3864 Girard Ave, Culver City 310 837 7795

Michael Rudin*
8132 W. 3rd St, LA 323 658 7601

J. Robert Scott* (trade only)
8727 Melrose Ave, W. Hollywood 310 659 4910

Eric Zammit (elegant minimalism)
323 E. Altadena Dr, Altadena 626 398 9309

Furniture, Contemporary & Classic Modern

Dakota Jackson* (trade only)
Pacific Design Center 310 659 7424

Diva*
8801 Beverly Blvd, LA 310 278 3191

ICF*
1343 4th St, Santa Monica 310 260 9516

Janus et Cie* (trade only)
Pacific Design Center 310 652 7090

Knoll* (moving to Santa Monica)
Pacific Design Center 310 289 5800

Linea*
8843 Beverly Blvd, LA 310 273 5425

Herman Miller* (office)
633 W. 5th St, LA 213 627 5900

Modern Living*
8775 Beverly Blvd, LA 323 657 8775

Palazetti*
9006 Beverly Blvd, LA 310 273 2225

SEE*
8806 Beverly Blvd, LA 310 385 1919

Jules Seltzer/Herman Miller for the Home*
8833 Beverly Blvd, LA 310 274 7243

Furniture, Vintage Modern

Blackman Cruz*
800 N. La Cienega Blvd, W. Hollywood 310 657 9228

Carla
7466 Beverly Blvd, LA 323 932 6064

Downtown*
719 N. La Cienega Blvd, W. Hollywood 310 652 7461

Emmerson Troop*
7957 Melrose Ave, W. Hollywood 323 653 9763

Fat Chance*
162 N. La Brea Ave, LA 323 930 1960

Harry Art Furniture*
8639 Venice Blvd, Culver City 310 559 7863

LA Modern Auctions*
8057 Beverly Blvd, LA 323 904 1950

Modern One*
7956 Beverly Blvd, LA 323 651 5082

Modernica*
7368 Beverly Blvd, LA 323 933 0383

Orange*
245 S. Robertson Blvd, Beverly Hills 310 652 5195

Outside*
442 N. La Brea Ave, LA 323 934 1254

Pegaso International
8117 Melrose Ave, W. Hollywood 323 655 8117

Russell Simpson*
8125 Melrose Ave, W. Hollywood 323 651 3992

Skank World*
7205 Beverly Bvd, LA 323 939 7858

Sonrisa*
7609 Beverly Blvd, LA 323 935 8438

Thanks for the Memories*
8319 Melrose Ave, W. Hollywood 323 852 9407

Twentieth*
8057 Beverly Blvd, LA 323 904 1200

Glass

Campbell Custom Glass
4845 Exposition Blvd, LA 323 735 1445

Glassworks
7720 S. San Pedro St, LA . . .323 789 7800/323 846 1570

Pulps Studio (slump & laminated)
3105 S. La Cienega Blvd, LA 310 815 4999

Western Glass (discount)
3740 Fruitland Ave, Maywood 213 589 5461

Hardware

B & B
12450 W. Washington Blvd, LA 310 390 9413

Berg Hardware
495 N. Altadena Dr, Pasadena 626 793 6161

Carter Hardware
153 N. Robertson Blvd, Beverly Hills 310 657 1940

Design Hardware*
6053 3rd St, LA .323 930 1330

Details*
8625 ½ Melrose Ave, W. Hollywood 310 659 1550

Liz's Antique Hardware*
435 S. La Brea Ave, LA 323 939 4403

Interdisciplinary Design

Forms & Surfaces*
Pacific Design Center 310 659 9134

Susan Frank & David Frisch
125 E. Linden Ave, Burbank 818 557 1318

Hedge Design Collective
5727 Venice Blvd, LA 323 954 9084

Lisa Krohn, Krohn Design
1304 N. Beverly Glen Blvd, LA 310 470 3597

Stuart Kurten Design
4204 Glencoe Ave, Marina del Rey 310 827 8722

Simon Maltby (glass, bathtubs, etc.)
519 Santa Clara, Venice 310 392 2588

Kitchens

Bulthaup*
153 S. Robertson Blvd, LA 310 288 3875

Cooper-Pacific Kitchens* (trade only)
Pacific Design Center 800 743 6284

Kitchen Design Studio
400 N. Robertson Blvd, LA 310 854 6322

Poggenpohl* (trade only)
Pacific Design Center 310 289 4901

Snaidero International* (trade only)
Pacific Design Center 310 657 5497

Kitchenware & Stoves

Antique Stove Heaven*
5414 S. Western Ave, LA 213 298 5581

Surfas (restaurant supplies)
8825 National Blvd, Culver City 310 559 4770

Lighting

Diva/Fontana d'Arte*
8801-3 Beverly Blvd, LA 310 278 3191

Highlights*
2435 Main St, Santa Monica 310 450 5886

Lampa
8317 Beverly Blvd, LA 323 852 1542

Plug*
8017 Melrose Ave, W. Hollywood 323 653 5635

Linens

Anichini*
466 N. Robertson Blvd, W. Hollywood 310 657 4292

Dormire*
1345 4th St, Santa Monica 310 393 9288

Frette*
449 N. Rodeo Dr, Beverly Hills 310 273 8540

International Down & Linen* (trade only)
Pacific Design Center 310 657 8243

Pratesi*
9024 Burton Way, Beverly Hills 310 274 7661

Room with a View
1600 Montana Ave, Santa Monica 310 998 5858

Shaxted
350 N. Camden Dr, Beverly Hills 310 273 4320

Markets

Pasadena City College Flea Mkt (1st Su, lot 1)
1570 E. Colorado Blvd, Pasadena 626 585 7906

Rose Bowl Flea Mkt (2nd Su)
1001 Rose Bowl Dr, Pasadena 626 588 4411

Antique & Collectible Mkt (3rd Su)
Veterans Memorial Stadium, Conant St. (between
Lakewood & Clark), Long Beach 310 655 5703

Antique & Collectible Mkt (4th Su)
Airport Ave, off Bundy, Santa Monica 310 933 2511

LA Modernism Show (May)
Santa Monica Civic Auditorium 310 455 2886

Santa Monica Antique Market
1607 Lincoln Blvd, Santa Monica 310 314 4899

Metalworkers

Gianni Bodo
2977 La Castana Dr, LA 323 874 5693

Du Rovan
5009 Exposition Blvd, LA 323 732 9797

Tom Farrage
8557 Higuera St, Culver City 310 842 9884

Murray's Iron Works
8632 Melrose Ave, W. Hollywood 310 839 7739

John Stiebel, Art Metal
16823 S. Broadway, Gardena 310 327 1129

Sallie Trout, Trout Studios
5880 Blackwelder St, Culver City 310 202 8868

Papers

Hiromi Papers*
Bergamot Station, Santa Monica 310 998 0098

Claudia Laub
7404 Beverly Blvd, LA 323 931 1710

McManus & Morgan*
2506 W. 7th St, LA 213 387 4433

Soolip*
8646 Melrose Ave, W. Hollywood 310 360 0545

Soolip-Marie Papier*
8574 Melrose Ave, W. Hollywood 310 360 0581

Photography Galleries

Apex Fine Art*
332 La Brea Ave, LA 323 634 7887

Stephen Cohen*
7358 Beverly Blvd, LA 323 937 5525

Fahey-Klein*
148 N. La Brea Blvd, LA 323 934 2250

Peter Fetterman*
Bergamot Station, Santa Monica 310 453 6463

G. Ray Hawkins*
908 Colorado Blvd, Santa Monica 310 394 5558

Jan Kesner*
164 N. La Brea Blvd, LA 323 938 6834

Paul Kopeikin*
138 N. La Brea Ave, LA 323 937 0765

Craig Krull*
Bergamot Station, Santa Monica 310 828 6410

rosegallery*
Bergamot Station, Santa Monica 310 264 8440

Picture Framers

Aesthetic Frame & Art Services*
8221 Melrose Ave, W. Hollywood 323 653 9033

Art Concepts*
Bergamot Station, Santa Monica 310 315 9772

Art Exchange
2451 Broadway, Santa Monica 310 828 6866

Boris
305 N. Robertson Blvd, Beverly Hills 310 275 8312

Jeffrey Kies
2236 Ronda Vista Dr, LA 323 662 9304

Sherman Galleries
4039 Lincoln Blvd, Marina del Rey 310 305 1001

Jerry Solomon
960 N. La Brea Ave, LA 323 851 7241

Plastics

Hastings Plastics
1704 Colorado Ave, Santa Monica 310 829 3449

Plastic Mart
2101 Pico Blvd, Santa Monica 310 451 1701

Solter Plastics
12016 Pico Blvd, W. LA 310 473 5115

Plumbing Fixtures

Ardy Bath Collection
8665 Wilshire Blvd, Beverly Hills 310 659 8800

Rombord Sax
8904 Beverly Blvd, LA 310 550 1070

Snyder Diamond
1399 Olympic Blvd, Santa Monica 310 277 8978

Waterworks* (also Pasadena & Newport Beach)
8715 Melrose Ave, W. Hollywood 310 289 5211

Premium Outlet Stores

Camarillo Premium Outlets
850 Ventura Blvd, Camarillo 805 445 8520

Desert Hills Premium Outlets
48400 Seminole Dr, Cabazon 909 849 6641

Stone & Tile

Ceramic Tile Center
2001 Westwood Blvd, W. LA 310 470 6629

Gosford Quarries (Australian sandstone)
7763 Lemona Ave, Van Nuys 818 909 6600

Mission Tile West* (also Pasadena & Newport Beach)
853 Mission St, Pasadena 626 799 4595

Ann Sacks* (also Pasadena & Newport Beach)
8483 Melrose Ave, W. Hollywood 323 658 8884

Syndesis* (Syndecrete)
2908 Colorado Ave, Santa Monica 310 829 9932

Walker & Zanger* (also Pasadena & Newport Beach)
8750 Melrose Ave, W. Hollywood 310 659 1234

Index of Architects/Designers

Index of Architects/Designers

Credits

Author
Michael Webb

Publisher/Creative Director
Mark Johnson

Editors
Kathleen duBois
Laura Stern

Design
Annette Krammer
Erik Tomita

Production Coordinator
Kathleen duBois

Cartography
Patricia Keelin

Photography
Erhard Pfeiffer

Sales
Kathleen duBois
Laura Stern

Printing/Film Production
John Skinner- Press Check Inc., San Francisco, CA

Michael Webb is executive editor of the **Architecture + Design** series, and writes on these subjects for leading magazines around the world. His 15 books include four monographs on residential architecture, **Architects House Themselves: Breaking New Ground, The City Square, Through the Windows of Paris: 50 Unique Shops, It's a Great Wall!,** and an upcoming study of mid-century modern American houses. He was born in London and has lived in Los Angeles for 23 years in the Neutra apartment that Charles and Ray Eames called home through the '40s.

Mark Johnson, AIA, is President and Creative Director of The**Understanding**Business (T**U**B), an Information Design and Publishing firm in the Bay Area. With his formal training and experience in architecture, Johnson co-founded T**U**B in 1987 to apply architectural principles to the design of information. T**U**B has since created extraordinary guides to such diverse subjects as architecture, cities, sports, and finance. T**U**B has also created the Pacific Bell Smart™ Yellow Pages in California, and designed and produced many of the ACCESS® travel guides for US and worldwide destinations. T**U**B is positioned to assist corporations in a variety of new ways, including information architecture, strategic design planning, and the creation of innovative print and electronic products. As T**U**B continues to grow, it is constantly in search of better ways of *communicating ideas and information*℠.

The**Understanding**Business®
901 Grayson Street, Suite 201 Berkeley, CA 94710
TEL 510 649 3730 FAX 510 649 3738
NET www.tub.com   E-MAIL kdubois@tub.com

ISBN 0-9641863-6-5

Third Edition, Copyright© The**Understanding**Business Press, a division of The**Understanding**Business. All rights reserved. No portion of this publication may be reproduced or transmitted in any form or manner by any means, including, but not limited to, graphic, electronic, and mechanical methods, photocopying, recording, taping, or any informational storage and retrieval system without explicit permission from the publisher. The publisher and the author assume no legal responsibility for the completeness or accuracy of the contents of this book, nor any legal responsibility for the appreciation or depreciation in the value of any products, commercial or otherwise, by reason of inclusion or exclusion from this book. All contents are based on information available at the time of publication.